Foreword

When you grow up in London, the only walking you do is to the local market, park, or school. When you do venture from your neighbourhood, you're usually staring down from the top deck of a double decker bus at identical rows of terraced housing, or seeing the carriage doors of the tube opening and closing on the same station names that you've passed a hundred times before. For years, my geographic understanding of my hometown was predicated on the colourful line drawings of Mr. Harry Beck, who designed our tube map. Years later, when I began working and earning money, I moved from south to southwest to west London, but, honestly, my pattern didn't vary much. I would walk to do my shopping nearby or head into the West End on public transport. That all changed one day when a Czech friend – who had been living in London for many years – invited me to go for a stroll.

That was more than ten years ago. Along the way, we passed by the alabaster townhouses and mews streets of Kensington before entering the mystery that was Leighton House. Over the ensuing months, we would meet up most mornings, for an hour before work, and walk. Until then, I hadn't truly understood what it was to attend to a thing: be it a moment, a season, or a place. Now, whenever I need to clear my head, a walk is the surest way to revive my spirits.

Within these pages, I've tried to both share a sense of the city's scale and diversity, and zoom in on the ambience and character of clusters of neighbourhoods. The truth is, Londoners (whether they are born here, live and work here, or raise families here) are part of a great, fabled city. We're told stories all day long about what it means to live in a certain postcode, or to say you're from north or south of the river; but what I would wish for you on these walks is the freedom of crossing borders, kicking allegiances to the kerb, and discovering how no one district has a monopoly on the city's identity.

I can only hope, by the end, that you are as smitten by London as I continue to be.

– Nicola Perry

33 Walks

CENTRAL
LONDON

1 The Luxury Seekers' Walk

Mayfair

BEST TIME: Weekend morning
DISTANCE: Approximately 4.5 kilometres

Wandering around Mayfair, what impresses me most is the area's celebration of tradition and quality. Look upward and you'll find the coats of arms and "Royal Warrant by Appointment" on companies' hoardings. Touchingly, I think of generations of tailors, shoemakers, perfumers, and jewellers whose services have been singled out by the Queen, becoming part of a centuries-old society. Whilst it is inevitable that you'll encounter retail stores on this walk, I want to draw your attention to the men and women, artisans and craftspeople, tradesmen and merchants, whose talents and hard graft have made possible what you see and touch today.

From Green Park Station, let's escape the shopping crowd and withdraw to a more discrete London, one experienced by royalty and aristocrats of old. Unless you're a local in the know, only by chance would you come upon ❶ SHEPHERD MARKET. Tucked down White Horse Road, off of Piccadilly, this is a charming piazza with a warren of streets, which even Google Maps street view cannot access. In the 1920s, Shepherd Market was considered to be London's most fashionable and opulent district by the city's bourgeois social elite. By the 1970s, it had more salacious connections with politicians and was the setting for rock star Keith Moon's fatal overdose. Today, it's a mix of eclectic cuisines, 18th-century pubs, and discreet residences. It's easy to walk right past notable restaurants, given their unassuming exteriors. There are many excellent options, but for a real culinary twist, check out Polish-Mexican bistro ❷ L'AUTRE. Brimming with personality, it's a kitschy blend of authentic timber beams, an electric fire straight out of the 1970s, and an absurd, fun mix of

Opposite: James Purdey & Sons

Above: Church of the Immaculate Conception, Mount Street Gardens; Below: Carlos Place

paraphernalia. As in all the best little places, the proprietor and staff treat you like an old friend. Return here at lunch or suppertime to soak up the ambience.

Pushing on, head for Curzon Street by way of Hertford Street and turn right on South Audley. A quiet road, it is lined with grand mansion blocks – former aristocratic residences, no less. Be on the lookout for the giant twin ceramic elephants that stand sentinel at No. 19. This is ❶ THOMAS GOODE & CO., a celebrated supplier of china, glassware, and silver whose prestigious clients have included the Russian tsar and Queen Victoria. With its 13 showrooms filled with various table arrangements, it is worth visiting for the setting alone. A few doors away is ❷ GROSVENOR CHAPEL. I am particularly fond of the Dutch-looking building tucked alongside. For those of you in search of Royal Warrant holders, though, you couldn't do better than ❸ JAMES PURDEY & SONS, up ahead at No. 57, which has been making bespoke guns for nearly two centuries and possesses not one but three Royal Warrants.

Turning away from merchandise for a moment, you'll find an oasis of serenity mere steps away. Behind Grosvenor Chapel and protected by a wall of mansion blocks is Mount Street Gardens, an attractive open space with large London plane trees and ornamental lawns. Tucked in a corner is the ❹ FARM STREET CHURCH, a 200-year-old Gothic Revival church, which still holds a Latin mass for worshippers.

Exit the gardens at Mount Street, opposite the church, and give a passing nod to the Connaught Hotel, where a room will set you back at least £1000 a night. Just up ahead, look to the right, and you'll see on the corner, ❺ SCOTT'S, one of the best fish restaurants in London and among the few to offer outdoor dining, which leads us to its other claim to fame, or shame: Charles Saatchi, being a fan of both seafood and smoking, would often dine here; and Scott's became the scene of his horrendous and rather public fights with his wife, Nigella Lawson.

At this junction, you could wend your way to Berkeley Square and on to old and new Bond Streets, but instead I will lead you up Davies Street and steer you right on Brook Street. A remarkable facet to London is how craftsmen and artisans cluster together, remaining indomitably loyal to a neighbourhood, and often a single street. For guitar sellers in London, that street was Tin Pan Alley; for tailors, it is still Savile Row; and for art dealers, it is Brook Street and its environs. (Most famously, Mayfair is home to the art auctioneers Sotheby's at 34-35 New Bond Street). Brook Street is also known for ❽ CLARIDGE'S HOTEL, whose storied past reaches back more than 150 years. But you'd have to be in the know to stumble upon ❾ LANCASHIRE COURT. I won't spoil the surprise, but best to duck down this hidden passageway in the early evening to enjoy the convivial bar atmosphere. Also, for a special treat, I entreat you to head to ❿ PENHALIGON'S perfumers at 20a Brook Street, not just for its scents but also for its history, which is expertly divulged by the store's knowledgeable staff.

Continuing on Brook Street, you'll pass Fenwick department store on your right and Hanover Square on your left before reaching Regent Street. Turn right on Regent and then take the first left onto Great Marlborough Street. A walking tour of this neighbourhood would be incomplete without a stop at the corner of Kingly Street, where the Grade II-listed ⓫ LIBERTY LONDON building has stood since 1924.

Alongside Fortnum & Mason, no other department store in London transports you back so remarkably to an earlier era. The mock-Tudor building is constructed from the timbers of two ships – the HMS *Impregnable* and the HMS *Hindustan* – and the attention to detail is breathtaking. Inside is a veritable emporium selling everything from perfumes to printed fabric scarves to the smallest haberdashery items. What sets it apart, though, is both its homey feel – there are original fireplaces in many of the rooms – and the approachable staff, who exhibit a genuine interest and pride in their wares. Liberty is also known for its history of working with great

Clockwise from top left: Claridge's hotel;
Penhaligon's perfumiers; Lancashire
Court; Liberty London department store;
restaurants lining Lancashire Court;
Savile Row shop window

Above: Carnaby Street; Below: Savile Row street sign

designers – from William Morris and Dante Gabriel Rossetti in the 19th century to Yves Saint Laurent and Dame Vivienne Westwood in the 20th. Come the 1960s, the store experienced something of a renaissance, with designers like Mary Quant and Jean Muir producing the shop's signature line of fabrics.

Leave by the Carnaby Street exit and you are in one of the more youthful shopping corridors of London Town. The street's reputation was sealed back in the swinging sixties, when fashion designer Mary Quant opened her shop here, and the Who's Pete Townshend, the Jam's Paul Weller, and Jimi Hendrix all became regular fixtures.

But for a glimpse into another bygone world, which has experienced something of a revival, your next stop must be the golden mile of men's tailoring: Savile Row. From Carnaby Street, turn right onto Beak Street and right again at Regent Street; then take the first left onto New Burlington Street, and left again onto Savile Row. Make your way to ⊕ HUNTSMAN & SONS at No. 11. Entering this shop is more like being welcomed into a gentlemen's club than a mere men's clothing store. Here, the client is always "sir," and it's easy to picture former patrons Winston Churchill, Lord Nelson, and Charlie Chaplin, cane twirling, strolling in, even today. Weekdays at the back of Huntsman may well find a number of impeccably dressed tailors cutting cloth on wooden workbenches much like it has been done for 100 years.

From here, turn into Burlington Gardens, which backs onto the ⊕ ROYAL ACADEMY OF ARTS. A striking 17th-century mansion nestled in the heart of Mayfair, it hosts some of the finest arts exhibitions in London. Avoid the temptation to walk through Burlington Arcade (an upmarket pedestrian shopping corridor under a glazed roof), and keep moving on to the next corner, where Old and New Bond Streets meet. This route became hugely popular with upper-class residents as a place to socialize in the 18th century, and prestigious and expensive shops were soon established here. Ever since, this locale has held its reputation as *the* fashionable place for high-end retail, and is one of the most sought after strips of real estate in Europe.

More quintessentially English than shopping, however, is afternoon tea. This is something of a cultural tradition amongst the English upper classes. Nearby, both the Ritz hotel and Fortnum & Mason put on a fine spread of finger sandwiches and scones amidst elegant surroundings, but my personal recommendation is the

Above: A traditional city lamppost

⑭ ENGLISH TEA ROOM at Brown's Hotel around the corner on Albemarle Street (it is cosier and more intimate). In a city of 8.5 million, though, it is best to make a reservation in advance.

There are two more places of note along the way to Green Park Station that I would like to share. The first is Berkeley Square (pronounced BARK-lee), one of those splendid town squares that pop up on a London walk. This one has been the setting for London Fashion Week and its grand marquee until recently. Many of the town houses that you see here would have opened their doors for after-show parties inviting in the world's fashionistas.

This area has a reputation for private members' clubs, and one of its most famous is just off the square at Fitzmaurice Place. The interior of the ⑮ LANSDOWNE CLUB combines 18th-century grandeur with Art Deco design. Built in 1763 as a private residence, the architecturally exquisite house was established as a social club in 1935.

Whilst this walk doesn't grant you a pass into the inner enclaves of London society, I hope, as you stroll back around to Green Park, you have a greater sense of the craftspeople, merchants, and society folk who make London what it is.

Pavement seating in front of L'Autre

Green Park Underground Station

GETTING THERE

Victoria/Jubilee/Piccadilly Lines

1 SHEPHERD MARKET

Mayfair, London W1J 7QU
www.shepherdmarket.co.uk

2 L'AUTRE

5b Shepherd Street
London W1J 7HP
+44 20 7499 4680

3 THOMAS GOODE & CO

19 S Audley Street
London W1K 2BN
+44 20 7499 2823
www.thomasgoode.com

4 GROSVENOR CHAPEL

24 S Audley Street
London W1K 2PA
+44 20 7499 1684
www.grosvenorchapel.org.uk

5 JAMES PURDEY & SONS

57–58 S Audley Street
London W1K 2ED
+44 20 7499 1801
www.purdey.com

6 FARM STREET CHURCH

114 Mount Street
London W1K 3AH
+44 20 7493 7811
www.farmstreet.org.uk

7 SCOTT'S

20 Mount Street
London W1K 2HE
+44 20 7495 7309
www.scotts-restaurant.com

8 CLARIDGE'S

Brook Street, London W1K 4HR
+44 20 7629 8860
www.claridges.co.uk

9 LANCASHIRE COURT
Brook Street, London W1S 1EY

10 PENHALIGON'S

20A Brook Street, London W1K 5DE
+44 20 7493 0002
www.penhaligons.com

11 LIBERTY LONDON

Regent Street, London W1B 5AH
+44 20 7734 1234
www.liberty.co.uk

12 HUNTSMAN & SONS

11 Savile Row, London W1S 3PS
+44 20 7734 7441
www.huntsmansavilerow.com

13 ROYAL ACADEMY OF ARTS

Burlington House
London W1J 0BD
+44 20 7300 8090
www.royalacademy.org.uk

14 BROWN'S HOTEL

Brown's Hotel, 33 Albemarle Street
London W1S 4BP
+44 20 7493 6020
www.roccofortehotels.com

15 THE LANSDOWNE CLUB

9 Fitzmaurice Place
London W1J 5JD
+44 20 7629 7200
www.lansdowneclub.com

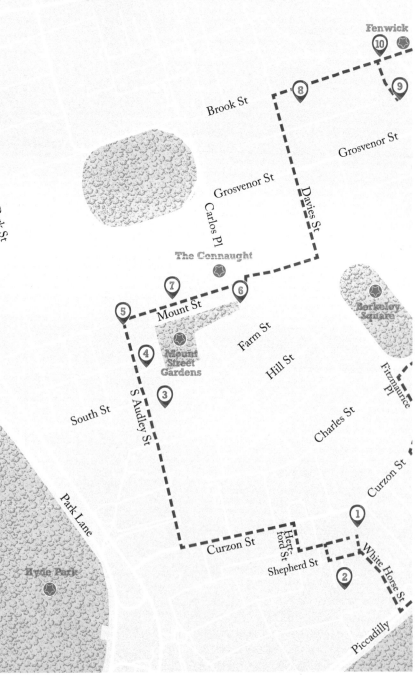

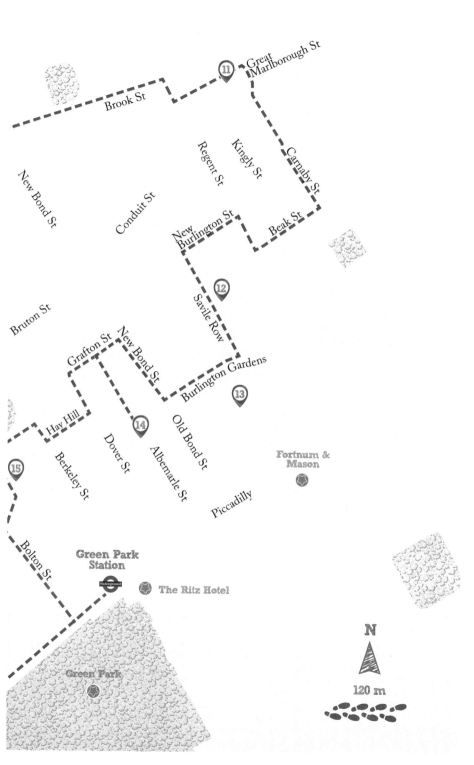

2___The Promenade Walk
South Bank to Bankside

BEST TIME: Sunrise or sunset
DISTANCE: Approximately 5 kilometres

Crossing the Golden Jubilee Bridge from Embankment to South Bank, you instantly feel more alive with the wind blowing across your cheeks and the sight of the London Eye at the river's bend. While others stop to appreciate the city's skyline, my stride always lengthens – accelerates even – as if I were urgently needed to assume my place on the other side. For nowhere else in London offers more sundry entertainment than this famed stretch of riverfront promenade. Step right up, folks, for the South Bank Experience: the greatest walk in town.

Look up in awe at the huge spinning disk that is the London Eye alongside the ❶ SOUTHBANK CENTRE, the largest collective arts complex in the world (including the Royal Festival Hall, Hayward Gallery, Queen Elizabeth Hall, Purcell Room, and Poetry Library). Thanks to investment in the area, the more brutal aspect to this 1960s concrete construction has lost some of its severity with the arrival of upscale chain restaurants, making this one of the buzziest dining hotspots in town. As with a funhouse, your South Bank walk is a participatory experience, in which you'll encounter spectacles designed to surprise and amuse you. First though I recommend maintaining a steady course across the centre's mezzanine level. Down the steps, in back, you'll find a lively courtyard food market, where you can sample some of the best street food and produce in the capital.

Cutting back to the river through the ❷ ROYAL FESTIVAL HALL, renowned for world music, I always make a point to head to the fourth floor via the lift, as the main foyer staircases seem more

Opposite: Book market under Waterloo Bridge

Above: View of St Paul's Cathedral; Below: The Skatepark at Southbank

designed to befuddle than smoothly lead you through the building. From here, you are afforded one of the best free views in London. To the west is Westminster Abbey and the London Eye, and, to the east, St Paul's and Mary's Axe, colloquially known as the Gherkin because of its distinctive shape, which many agree resembles a pickled cucumber. Venture up the maze-like stairs of the Festival Hall to the Poetry Library on level five, where you can request an audio recording of such 20th-century poets as Sylvia Plath or Ted Hughes, pull on a set of headphones, sit back, close your eyes, and imagine you're in the room with them.

Outside again at river level, eyes wide open, look out for people loitering below ❸ QUEEN ELIZABETH HALL, which hosts daily classical, jazz, and avant-garde music and dance performances. On first inspection, the presence of this graffiti-covered underpass packed with freewheeling skateboarders may seem incongruous with the concert venue above, but the fact that the walls of the self-appointed ❹ SKATEPARK have not been whitewashed is a testament to the cultural base here. Instead, the park has been embraced as part of the performance scene. Another sport to look out for is *parkour*, with young people jumping through the air from pillar to post in terrifying feats of human daring – just be sure you're not under one of them. Did you happen to look up? If so, you would have spotted a most curious sight: a houseboat, of all things, moored on the roof of Queen Elizabeth Hall. The installation was inspired by – and named after – Joseph Conrad's ❺ ROI DES BELGES, which he navigated up the River Congo before penning *Heart of Darkness*. There's a logbook on the bridge where overnight guests are each invited to record their individual experience of the city from the vantage point of the suspended boat.

Moving along the promenade towards Waterloo Bridge, you'll soon reach the ❻ BRITISH FILM INSTITUTE, which shows movies from all over the world – in particular, critically acclaimed foreign, historical, and specialized films. Underneath the bridge, come rain or shine, you'll also find one of the best outdoor book markets in London. With views of Gothic-style buildings on the other side of the river, reminiscent of the Seine, the scene has a rather Parisian aspect.

Leaving behind the Southbank Centre and ❼ NATIONAL THEATRE (a strikingly brutalist structure where 30 productions are staged each year – everything from Greek tragedy and Shakespeare to modern masterpieces and new works by contemporary writers and theatre-makers), you'll soon spot the Elizabethan warehouses up ahead. For this whole area used to be wharves, with as many as 1,700 lining the bank of the River Thames. The docks once thrived with the bustle and commerce of handling valuable cargoes from Europe, the West Indies, Africa, and the Far East. Today, you'll find ❽ GABRIEL'S WHARF, a small crafty enclave, home to a mix of independent shops, cafes, bars, and restaurants. Alongside, there's the ❾ OXO TOWER, which was largely rebuilt to an Art Deco design between 1928 and 1929. The story goes that the owner of OXO wanted to include a tower featuring illuminated signs advertising the name of their product. When permission for the advertisements was refused, the tower was built with four sets of three vertically stacked windows, which "coincidentally" happened to form a circle, a cross, and a circle.

What I personally love about this area is how visionaries have transformed the former warehouses into all types of creative spaces, from Michelin-starred restaurants to arthouse cinemas to pop-up performance venues. I still fondly recall attending a participatory theatre experience of *Alice in Wonderland* at ❿ BARGEHOUSE. One whole floor of the building was set up for the Mad Hatter's tea party while the most popular room was the smallest of them all. Inside the packed space, fully grown audience members sat cross-legged on the floor, captivated by the riddles of a thespian dressed up as the Caterpillar.

Pass under Blackfriars Bridge next, and you are entering Shakespeare territory. Across the Thames, the playwright once lived and wrote in a garret along Ireland Yard, down from St Paul's Cathedral, whilst

Clockwise from top left: OXO Tower; skateboarder at Southbank Skatepark; Gabriel's Wharf – row of independent shops and boutiques, The Wharf restaurant, characterful street art; London Eye

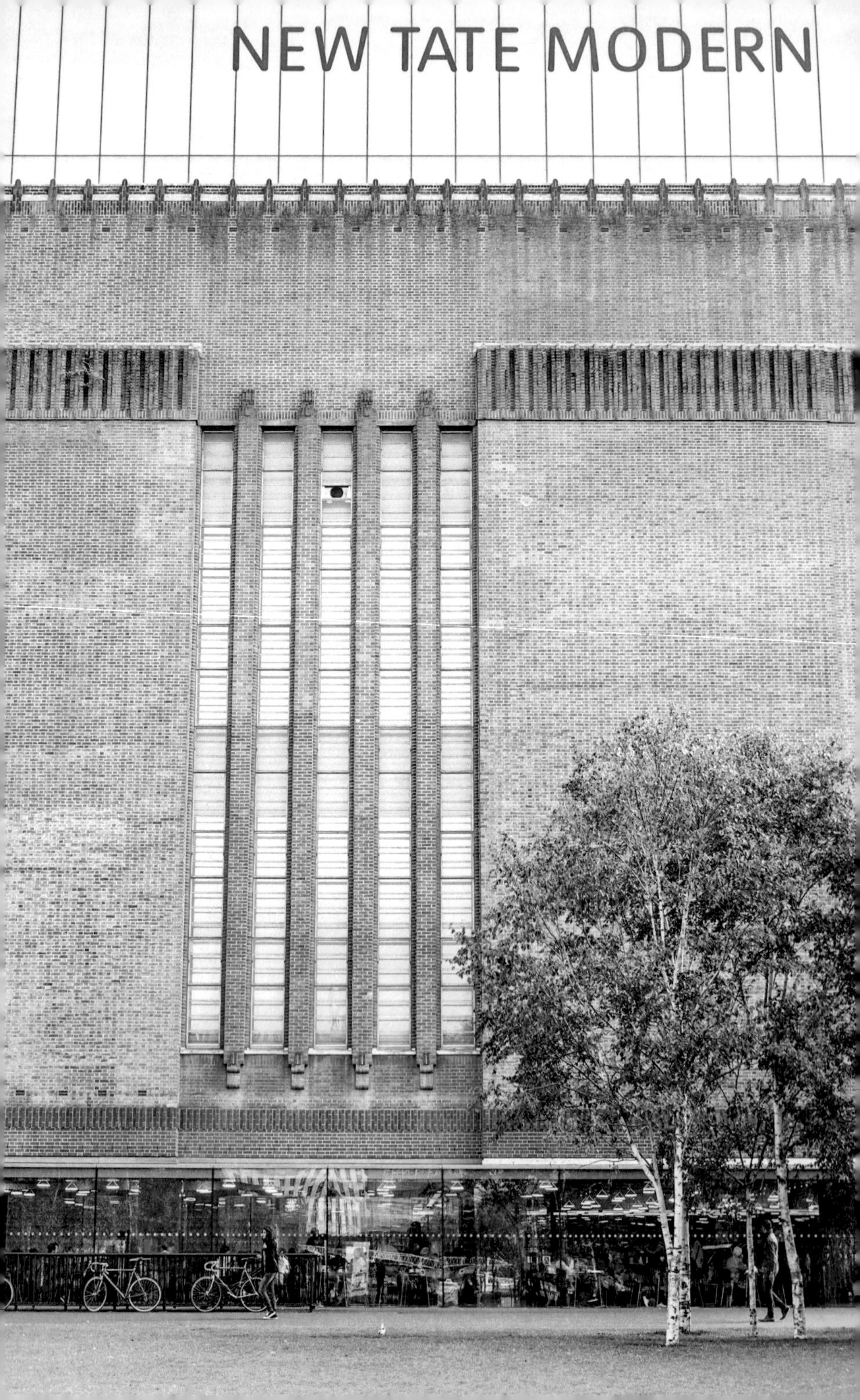
NEW TATE MODERN

Above: The Globe Theatre

farther along the South Bank, you will encounter a reconstruction of Shakespeare's Elizabethan playhouse, the ⑫ GLOBE THEATRE, where the Bard's works were performed until the original building burned down, 350 years ago. Before reaching the Globe, however, there's the ⑪ TATE MODERN, the grand industrial building turned Britain's national gallery of international modern art – and London's pride and joy.

Continue on, and below the train tracks you'll hear patrons of the ⑬ ANCHOR BANKSIDE pub sitting and joking outside the large seating area provided. While the railway lines above somewhat curtail the view, the spiritedness of the area more than compensates. If you do stop off for liquid refreshment, it may interest you to know the location's more macabre past. As well as being the site of a Roman grave and plague pits during 1603, it was also the place where Samuel Pepys watched the Great Fire in 1666. Pause for a moment – riverside – to drink in the view of the turrets of the great Tower of London, the dome of St Paul's Cathedral, and the shining skyscrapers across the waters. Wouldn't you agree the capital truly is a marvellous place?

From here, the streets leading off from Bankside – particularly Clink Street – eschew the bright lights of the city to offer a counterpoint with a more shadowy, atmospheric "ye olde England" feel. Follow Clink Street to its end and you'll come upon a replica of Sir Francis Drake's ship, the ⑭ GOLDEN HINDE II, docked in a small estuary. Move up Cathedral Street, and you're soon at ⑮ BOROUGH MARKET, the liveliest and most lauded food emporium in town.

Opposite: Tate Modern

❶ SOUTHBANK CENTRE
Belvedere Road
London SE1 8XX
+44 20 7960 4200
www.southbankcentre.co.uk

❷ ROYAL FESTIVAL HALL
Southbank Centre
Belvedere Road
London SE1 8XX
+44 20 7960 4200
www.southbankcentre.co.uk

❸ QUEEN ELIZABETH HALL
Southbank Centre
Belvedere Road
London SE1 8XX
+44 844 875 0073
www.southbankcentre.co.uk

❹ SOUTHBANK SKATEPARK
(underneath Queen Elizabeth Hall)
London SE1 8XZ

❺ ROI DES BELGES
(on the roof of Queen Elizabeth Hall)
www.southbankcentre.co.uk

❻ BFI SOUTHBANK
Belvedere Road
London SE1 8XT
+44 20 7928 3232
www.bfi.org.uk

❼ NATIONAL THEATRE
Upper Ground
London SE1 9PX
+44 20 7452 3000
www.nationaltheatre.org.uk

❽ GABRIEL'S WHARF
56 Upper Ground
London SE1 9PP
www.coinstreet.org/who-we-are/
contact-us/gabriels-wharf/

❾ OXO TOWER
02 Barge House Street
London SE1 9GY
+44 20 7021 1686
www.oxotower.co.uk

❿ BARGEHOUSE
Oxo Tower Wharf
Barge House Street
London SE1 9PH
+44 20 7021 1686
www.oxotower.co.uk

⓫ TATE MODERN
Bankside, London SE1 9TG
+44 20 7887 8888
www.tate.org.uk

⓬ GLOBE THEATRE
21 New Globe Walk
London SE1 9DT
+44 20 7902 1400
www.shakespearesglobe.com

⓭ ANCHOR BANKSIDE
34 Park Street, London SE1 9EF
+44 20 7407 1577
www.taylor-walker.co.uk

⓮ GOLDEN HINDE II
Pickfords Wharf, Clink Street
London SE1 9DG
+44 20 7403 0123
www.goldenhinde.com

⓯ BOROUGH MARKET
8 Southwark Street
London SE1 1TL
+44 20 7407 1002
www.boroughmarket.org.uk

Opposite: **Millennium Bridge over the River Thames**

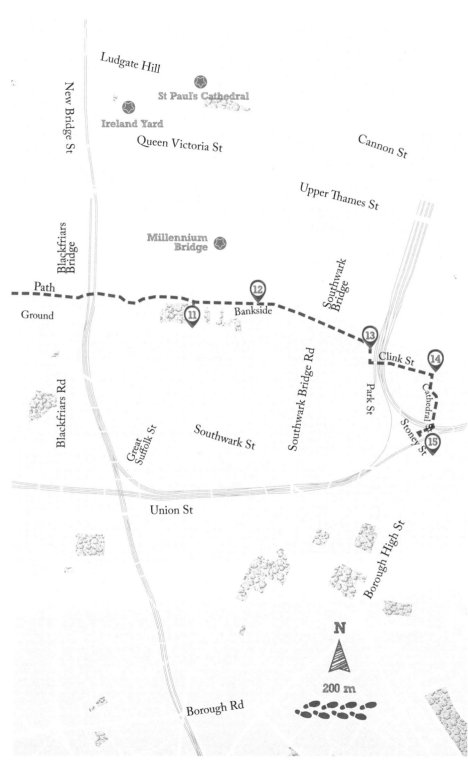

3__The Dickensian Walk

Russell Square to Temple

BEST TIME: Start out two hours before dusk
DISTANCE: Approximately 5 kilometres

Follow in the footsteps of Charles Dickens and walk the same streets he did as he dreamt up the characters and places for such classics as *Bleak House* and *Nicholas Nickleby*. Starting off at Russell Square, turn right out of the station and right again around Coram's Fields – a seven-acre recreational park – and left onto Guilford Street. Whilst there are still architectural elements of the foundling hospital that stood here for nearly 200 years, the building is long gone. But when Dickens lived in the neighbourhood, he would have looked through these same railings to the playground beyond, to see a multitude of orphans gathered up by philanthropist Captain Thomas Coram. The captain, appalled by the many homeless youths living in the streets, sought to build a "hospital for the maintenance and education of exposed and deserted young children." How fascinating to think that this place might have inspired Dickens to write *Oliver Twist*.

At Guilford and Doughty Streets, turn right and make your way to the ❶ **CHARLES DICKENS MUSEUM**, where the author once lived and rather impressively produced two books and two daughters in the space of two short years. Inside, you can wander through the various rooms and imagine Dickens pacing or brooding over manuscript pages.

From here, take the second right off Doughty Street onto North-ington, bearing right around to Rugby Street and then down to Lamb's Conduit Street. This partially pedestrianized street in Bloomsbury has established quite the reputation as a sophisticated hub for homegrown menswear. Local businesses cater to a rarefied

Opposite: Charles Dickens Museum

but loyal clientele, including surgeons from nearby Great Ormond Street Hospital and the lawyers of Lincoln's Inn (and, increasingly, folks from the worlds of advertising and architecture). Established as a local high street back in 1817, Lamb's Conduit has always had a distinct personality, proving a magnet for barristers since the 18th century. These days, it boasts an ethical supermarket/social enterprise, the People's Supermarket; a unique publishing house championing neglected female authors, Persephone Books; a bespoke tailors, Connock & Lockie, established in 1902; and the city's oldest undertakers, A. France & Son.

Turn left on Theobalds Road, and a few blocks down on the right you'll come to ❷ GRAY'S INN. Gray's is one of four Inns of Court in London. To be "called to the bar" and practise as a barrister in England and Wales, an individual must belong to one of these professional associations. For many years, Dickens studied law in this area, and would have had an intimate knowledge of the Inns, providing him with ample settings for his novels. This particular Inn is known for its gardens, which have existed since 1597, and Dickens is sure to have wandered through here many times. At the end of the 18th century, Charles Lamb described the gardens as the best of the four Inns of Court, "their aspect being altogether reverend and law-abiding." You too can access the gardens, along with residents and non-residents alike, between 12pm and 2:30pm on weekdays (public holidays excluded). Exit via Fulwood Place onto High Holborn to the south.

Close by is the former Furnival's Inn (now Holborn Bars) at 138–142 Holborn, where Dickens rented rooms from December 1834 and throughout the first year of his marriage, until 1837. He also began the *Pickwick Papers* whilst a tenant here. But for a more juridical walk, keep moving west by way of High Holborn and turn down Great Turnstile, where you'll enter a large garden square. This is Lincoln's Inn Fields.

Opposite: Connock & Lockie on Lamb's Conduit Street

On the north side of the Fields, you'll come upon ❸ SIR JOHN SOANE'S MUSEUM. Whilst the celebrated 19th-century architect Soane died in 1837 – the year Dickens moved to Doughty Street and the same year Victoria became Queen – the two men would both have known a time of heavy fogs, grime, and congested streets: the very image conjured up when you think of the word *Dickensian*. But step inside Soane's former family home, and you enter a radiant, bright environment. Soane designed the house in response to the dark and grim world outside, illuminating the interior in every imaginable way. Inside this extraordinary warren of rooms, a domed ceiling is capped with a delicate cupola of coloured glass, and there are mirrors everywhere.

Along Newman's Row, to the east of the Fields, you'll often find Bentleys parked up and chauffeurs shooting the breeze, although whether they are waiting for wealthy paying clients or highly paid lawyers depends on the occasion. Historically, the Inns – as opposed to the lowercase "inns" used by travellers and pilgrims – have been the houses of magnates of all kinds. The Inns offered overnight accommodations for visiting members, including statesmen, bishops, civil servants, and lawyers, whose business brought them to town, especially when Parliament and the courts were in session.

Dramatically different in style to Gray's Inn, which has a rather modest demeanour, ❹ LINCOLN'S INN is more medieval in aspect. Set within 11 acres, it is well known for its large garden and library, which date back to 1422. It is open to the public Monday through Friday from 7am to 7pm, and whilst I have only included the old and new squares on this walk, there are plenty of interesting offshoots within the grounds to discover at your own leisure.

The closer you move towards the Royal Courts of Justice, and the pub ❺ SEVEN STARS on Carey Street, the likelier you are to encounter members of our legal profession, absent their robes and wigs, propping up a very different kind of bar after a long day shuttling between their chambers and the courts. The surrounding neighbourhood is peppered generously with reminders of the pomp and ceremony of the English

Clockwise from top left: Lincoln's Inn; Royal Oak clock on John Street; Somerset House; The Seven Stars pub; The Devereux pub on Devereux Court; under Somerset House

BY APPOINTMENT TO
H.M. QUEEN ELIZABETH II
ROBE MAKERS & TAILORS
EDE AND RAVENSCROFT

courts. I particularly admire the regalia in the shopfront of ❻ EDE & RAVENSCROFT around the corner on Chancery Lane. Founded in 1689, this is London's oldest tailor and robe maker.

Take the shortcut through the grounds of the Maughan Library, housed in a 19th-century neo-Gothic building, and you are one street away from ❼ DR JOHNSON'S HOUSE. The beautifully restored 300-year-old town house is nestled on Gough Square amidst a maze of courts and alleys. It was here that Johnson compiled his great *Dictionary of the English Language*. Whilst Johnson and Dickens lived 100 years apart, they each had a love of night walking. Rumour has it that after killing off a major character, Dickens would stalk the streets until dawn as a way of easing his conscience.

By now, evening should be rolling in, so let's head inside, as Dickens surely would have done, to ❽ YE OLDE CHESHIRE CHEESE. Located on Fleet Street – once the epicentre of the newspaper trade – this has been a favourite watering hole of journalists and literary men for centuries. Johnson supped here, as did Voltaire, Thackeray, Pope, Conan Doyle, Mark Twain, W B Yeats, and Oscar Wilde. Once through the doors, you can appreciate what the draw has always been: higgledy-piggledy narrow passageways and staircases connecting a warren of bars and dining rooms, with dark wooden beams and low ceilings, open fireplaces, and a cosy atmosphere; best of all are the cavernous vaulted cellars dating back to a 13th-century Carmelite monastery.

Nearing the end of our Dickens-inspired walk, wander down Fleet Street passing the last two Inns of Court – Inner Temple and Middle Temple – accessible through the arched doorway in the Tudor-style building next to Wildy & Sons Ltd (16 Fleet Street). This is where Dickens studied the whole time he was writing *Bleak House*. Continue along Fleet Street toward the Royal Courts of Justice and take the left fork in the road, turning down Essex Street, passing by several law chambers, until you arrive at steps leading to the Thames. To reach Temple Underground, simply turn right along Temple Place.

Opposite: Ede & Ravenscroft, tailor and robe maker

Above: Royal Courts of Justice on the Strand

STARTING POINT
Russell Square Underground Station

GETTING THERE
Piccadilly Line

❶ CHARLES DICKENS MUSEUM
48 Doughty Street
London WC1N 2LX
+44 20 7405 2127
www.dickensmuseum.com

❷ GRAY'S INN
8 South Square
London WC1R 5ET
+44 20 7458 7800
www.graysinn.org.uk

❸ SIR JOHN SOANE'S MUSEUM
13 Lincoln's Inn Fields
London WC2A 3BP
+44 20 7405 2107
www.soane.org

❹ LINCOLN'S INN
Treasury Office
London WC2A 3TL
+44 20 7405 1393
www.lincolnsinn.org.uk

❺ SEVEN STARS
53 Carey Street
London WC2A 2JB
+44 20 7242 8521

❻ EDE & RAVENSCROFT
93 Chancery Lane
London WC2A 1DU
+44 20 7405 3906
www.edeandravenscroft.co.uk

❼ DR JOHNSON'S HOUSE
17 Gough Square, London EC4A 3DE
+44 20 7353 3745
www.drjohnsonshouse.org

❽ YE OLDE CHESHIRE CHEESE
145 Fleet Street, London EC4A 2BU
+44 20 7353 6170

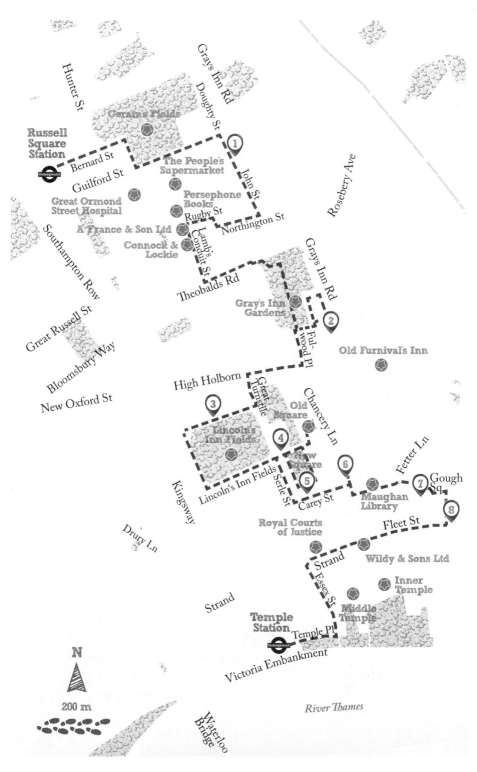

4 The Subterranean Walk

Vauxhall to Westminster to St James to Waterloo

BEST TIME: Anytime
DISTANCE: Approximately 7 kilometres

Delve into the backstreets of Millbank, Westminster, and St James's Park, and you are navigating areas that have been the seat of royal and parliamentary power for more than 900 years. With power comes subterfuge, though, and spooks (both the spying and supernatural kind) lie in wait behind even the plainest governmental buildings. This walk will take you underground, exploring the network of tunnels, centuries-old cellars, vaults, theatres, moats, and ruins that lurk beneath the shimmering surface.

Vauxhall hardly seems the most auspicious place to start a walk, with its multiple lanes of traffic, railway arches, and cranes towering over construction sites, but there's a reason I've brought you here first. Diagonally across from the subway entrance, you'll spot a Lego Land-like building – a fusion of Art Deco, classical, and industrial design elements. From the other side of the Thames, the building takes on an altogether different aspect, a facsimile perhaps of what an office block might look like if the Mayans were still around and erecting temples to corporate culture. This is in fact the ❶ MI6 HEADQUARTERS and, due to the sensitive nature of the secret intelligence service's work, large parts of the building are buried below street level. There's even speculation of a secret tunnel connecting MI6 to Whitehall, across the river.

My real motive for beginning here, however, is the rather incongruously positioned Georgian mansion located just a short walk from the station at 30 Wandsworth Road. Dwarfed by 21st-century high-rises that colonize the riverbanks, ❷ LASSCO BRUNSWICK HOUSE – set against the backdrop of brutalist

Opposite: LASSCO Brunswick House

Above: **MI6 Headquarters;** Below: **LASSCO Brunswick House**

railway arches and modernity – is easy to miss. For years, this building was used and abused by railway club members – who turned the grand salons into snooker halls – and later by squatters. But recently it has experienced something of a renaissance with the current proprietors, LASSCO (The London Architectural Salvage and Supply Co), who have brought their love of old buildings and architectural restoration to bear, showcasing the faded glory of this place. Step inside and wander through the tall salvaged doorway that connects the light and lofty parlour to the library, a room lined with tall cases of botanical books and brass foundry. Upstairs, tour the saloon with its open fires, green velvet curtains, and full-height windows. This was once the drawing room of the Duke of Brunswick and later the snooker room of the LSWR Scientific and Literary Institute. These days, the house is decorated with LASSCO's characteristically quirky stock of furniture, and much of what you see is for sale. Head down the cellar steps, your hand grazing the exposed 17th-century brickwork, before setting foot on the ancient flagstones, and explore the series of caves, sculleries, and pantries. Incredibly, the remains of the original 17th-century structure have been preserved, generating a spine-chilling experience.

Before you leave, be sure to check out the restaurant which is festooned with glamorous reclaimed décor, including walls covered in immense mirrors and a ceiling crammed to capacity with sparkling chandeliers. It's so over the top that you immediately feel at ease, recognizing the impish élan that has gone into every element of this fantastical venue.

Exiting Brunswick House, round the corner onto Nine Elms Lane and join the Riverside Walk heading to Vauxhall Bridge. Cross over the ancient River Effra and you'll reach Millbank, where in the 19th century, prisoners from Millbank Penitentiary would have boarded convict ships bound for Australia and faced a perilous and uncertain fate. Whilst others head up Millbank to the national art gallery, Tate Britain, our walk leads to the ❸ MORPETH ARMS. Here, you'll find abandoned prison cells in a dank basement corridor. Rumour has it that the pub's cellars are connected to an old passageway used by prisoners to escape from the penitentiary and avoid deportation.

Back outside in sunlight, continue along the grassy knoll to Victoria Tower Gardens and pass by the current HQ of ❹ MI5 – the UK's national security intelligence agency. On the far side of the gardens, turn onto Great College Street via the College Garden to access the grounds of the 700-year-old ❺ WESTMINSTER ABBEY. Rather macabre, the skeletons of 50 Londoners were found during routine maintenance work on the drainage pipes as recently as 2015.

As you stroll from the Abbey down Victoria Street, anyone would be hard-pressed to take in all the governmental buildings along the way, but worth noting are the apartment buildings filling the entire block between Dacre Street and Broadway. This site was once the iconic ❻ NEW SCOTLAND YARD building, headquarters of the Metropolitan Police Service. The real find, though, is tucked behind the Yard on Caxton Street, off Broadway, and that is the regal ❼ ST ERMIN'S HOTEL. During the Second World War, this was headquarters for covert operations, with MI6 and the Special Operations Executive relocating here. Ian Fleming and Kim Philby both worked in the building, while the hotel bar was one of Winston Churchill's favourite spots to meet with intelligence officers. Wherever you find spies (or spooks, as the Brits like to call them), you'll hear talk of secret passageways and, sure enough, there are tales of yet another subterranean tunnel, this one leading from under the hotel's grand staircase directly to Westminster.

Moving onward, turn your attention towards St James's Park and ❽ ST JAMES'S PALACE, where a passageway that dates from the Stuart era is said to run from the palace to a shop on the other side of Pall Mall. Rumour has it that Charles II would use it to slip across the road unnoticed into a nearby brothel. To reach the palace, head for St James's Park tube before turning right at the roundabout onto Queen Anne's Gate, and across the park. St James's Park is the oldest

Clockwise from top left: St James's Palace:
St James's Park; Riverside development,
Vauxhall; Queen Alexandra Monument
by Sir Alfred Gilbert, Marlborough Gate,
St James's Park; Diana Princess of Wales
Memorial Walk plaque, St James's Park;
LASSCO Brunswick House

of the capital's eight Royal Parks and is at the heart of ceremonial London, providing the setting for spectacular pageants, including the annual Trooping the Colour.

For those new to the city, St James's is the region of Westminster that encompasses Buckingham Palace and several discreetly located royal residences. At the Mall, cross over to Marlborough Road and continue on, passing the St James's Palace on your left. At the corner, take a left and head across Pall Mall to ❾ BERRY BROS & RUDD, a centuries-old wine merchant, on St James's Street. There are reports that down in its vast basement is a bricked-up archway facing the direction of the palace. Could this have been the very passage used by Charles II?

From here, walk along Cleveland Row to Stable Yard and ❿ CLARENCE HOUSE. This was home to Queen Elizabeth, the Queen Mother, for 50 years and is now the official residence of Charles, Prince of Wales. Access is prohibited with armed police guarding the perimeter. Keeping things in the family, it shares a garden with St James's Palace. It was here in June 1941 that representatives of the United Kingdom, Canada, Australia, New Zealand, the Union of South Africa, and the exiled European governments met and signed the Declaration of St James's Palace, which was the first of six treaties that established the United Nations.

Make your way back through St James's Park, and as you cross over the park's bridge for the second time, bear left, keeping the lake in plain sight, until you come to the first park exit onto Horse Guard's Road. Descend Clive Steps, and you are treading in the footsteps of Winston Churchill, who would shuffle underground into his World War II bunker during times of emergency. Today, the ⓫ CHURCHILL WAR ROOMS are a museum that honours the prime minister's life and legacy. Follow King Charles Street to Whitehall where the Ministry of Defence is located. (Its extensive network of underground tunnels is jokingly referred to as Q-Whitehall,

Opposite: Queen's Guard outside Clarence House

Above: Graffiti art in the tunnels under Waterloo Station

a nod to the James Bond franchise. What few people know is that Henry VIII's wine cellars are still below the stairs, although, sadly, they are closed to the public.) Turn right onto Parliament Street and then left across Westminster Bridge to Waterloo.

While nearby Southbank draws in the art crowds, and millions of commuters thump overhead on the concourse, below ground the alternative street scene holds court.

Make your way around the large roundabout, and the Park Plaza Hotel. At the first tunnel exit behind the hotel (with cars swooshing by), keep to the walkway and cut through to Station Approach and the ⑫ HOUSE OF VANS, where the cavernous tunnels have been repurposed into a skateboarding arena. This place is amazing. You can wander slap-bang into the grunge scene, and no one bats an eyelash. Continue to the underpass for Leake Street, and you'll enter a parallel universe where the smell of spray paint is overpowering and public-access tunnels are filled with street artists enjoying free license to paint the walls outside ⑬ THE VAULTS, an art hub nestled in the deep, dark tunnels under Waterloo Station. This vibe is a world away from St James, and makes for a potent contrast. From here, you can stroll up Station Approach and end the walk at Waterloo Station.

STARTING POINT
Vauxhall Underground Station

GETTING THERE
Victoria Line

Above: The Vaults art hub

1 MI6 HEADQUARTERS
85 Albert Embankment
London SE1 7TP
www.sis.gov.uk

2 LASSCO BRUNSWICK
HOUSE
30 Wandsworth Road
London SW8 2LG
+44 20 7394 2100
www.lassco.co.uk

3 MORPETH ARMS
58 Millbank, London SW1P 4RW
+44 20 7834 6442
www.morpetharms.com

4 MI5 HEADQUARTERS
Thames House, 12 Millbank
London SW1P 4QE
+44 20 7930 9000
www.mi5.gov.uk

5 WESTMINSTER ABBEY
20 Dean's Yard, London SW1P 3PA
+44 20 7222 5152
www.westminster-abbey.org

6 NEW SCOTLAND YARD
8–10 Broadway
London SW1H 0BG
+44 20 7230 1212
www.met.police.uk

7 ST ERMIN'S HOTEL
2 Caxton Street, London SW1H 0QW
+44 20 7222 7888
www.marriott.com

8 ST JAMES'S PALACE
Marlborough Road
London SW1A 1BS
+44 20 7930 4832
www.royal.gov.uk

9 BERRY BROS & RUDD
3 St James's Street
London SW1A 1EG
+44 800 280 2440
www.bbr.com

10 CLARENCE HOUSE
Little St James's Street
London SW1A 1BA
+44 20 7766 7303
www.royalcollection.org.uk

11 CHURCHILL WAR ROOMS
Clive Steps
King Charles Street
London SW1A 2AQ
+44 20 7930 6961
www.iwm.org.uk

12 HOUSE OF VANS
Arches
228–232 Station Approach Road
London SE1 8SW
+44 20 7922 1180
www.houseofvanslondon.com

13 THE VAULTS
Leake Street
London SE1 7NN
+44 20 7401 9603
www.thevaults.london

Piccadilly

St James's St

Cleveland Row

⑨

Pall Mall

Marlborough Rd

⑧

Stable Yard

⑩

The Mall

Constitution Hill

Grosvenor Pl

The Mall

St James Park

Clive Steps

⑪

King Charles St

Mi D

Whiteha

Buckingham Gate

Queen Anne's Gate

Birdcage Walk

Parliame Square

Caxton St

⑦

Dacre St

Tothill St

⑥

Broad way

Victoria St

⑤

The College Garden

Great Peter St

Buckingham Palace Rd

Rochester Row

Horseferry Rd

Vauxhall Bridge Rd

John Islip St

Tate Britain

Millb

③

Vauxhall B

Lupus St

N

200 m

Riverside W

②

Nine Elms Ln

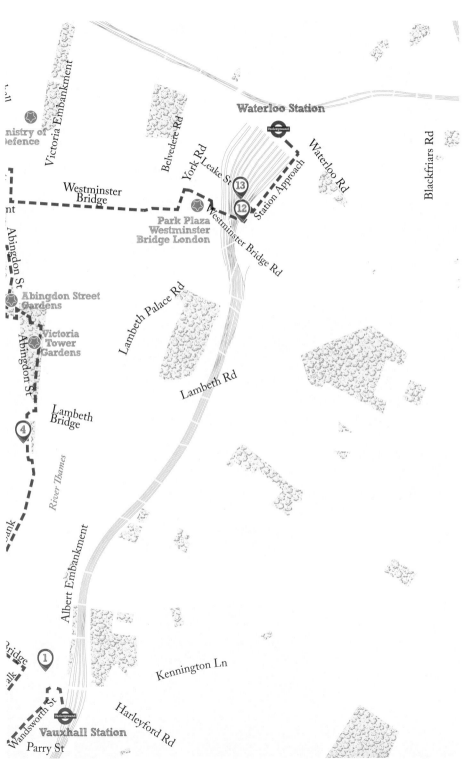

5__The Anti-Establishment Walk

Bloomsbury to Fitzrovia

BEST TIME: Spring or summer
DISTANCE: Approximately 5 kilometres

Home to the British Museum and University College London, Bloomsbury has become synonymous with a set of Cambridge intellectuals who, in the wake of the First World War, gathered together to discuss and debate philosophical and aesthetic ideas, often in the home of Virginia Woolf and her sister Vanessa Bell. Very much part of the "establishment," this group would also come to challenge social mores around homosexuality, feminism, and gender. It is this anti-establishment aspect to Bloomsbury that you'll encounter on this walk, which chronicles the area's past whilst initiating visitors into its quirky avant-gardism. Harbouring much more than meets the eye, this neighbourhood is full of surprises.

Whilst most visitors start out at Holborn and the British Museum, this walk begins at Russell Square. Turning away from UCL campus across the large square, turn down Herbrand Street on your left, towards the Friend at Hand pub on the corner of Colonnade. Adjacent is a sign for ❶ THE HORSE HOSPITAL. Built originally as stabling for cab drivers' sick horses, this hush-hush venue has played host to all manner of experimental and alternative artists since the 1990s, when stylist and costume designer Roger Burton opened it with an exhibition called "Vive Le Punk!" which was a retrospective of Vivienne Westwood's designs. To access the musty salon on the upper-floor ramp, you'll have to go up some hardwood slats, which were installed to prevent the horses from slipping. Burton & Co clearly have a tongue-in-cheek sense of humour, inviting you to

Opposite: The Horse Hospital

GREATER LONDON COUNCIL

Virginia
Stephen
(VIRGINIA WOOLF)
1882 ~ 1941
Novelist and Critic
lived here
1907 ~ 1911

Clockwise from top left: Charlotte Street;
Virginia Woolf blue plaque; Charlotte Street
Hotel; Wellcome Collection; Fitzroy Square

CHARLOTTE STREET HOTEL

become an ordained member of the Exclusive Grand Order of the Cobble when you sponsor one of more than 1000 cobblestones on Colonnade.

Double back on Herbrand Street in the direction from which you came, and make your way to No. 7. Incredibly, the 1930s Art Deco building you see before you started out as a garage and, after a dramatic redesign, became home to global ad agency ❷ MCCANN, which runs regular guided tours during Open House season (June).

Continue on into the heart of Bloomsbury. This is where the best-known members of the Bloomsbury Group – Virginia Woolf, John Maynard Keynes, E M Forster, and Lytton Strachey – met regularly, moving from square to square, house to house. Dorothy Parker once pithily described the group as "comprising pairs who had affairs in squares." Around the corner from McCann, on Tavistock Square, is the former ❸ HOME OF VIRGINIA WOOLF and her husband, Leonard. Virginia wrote most of her greatest novels here – *Mrs Dalloway*, *To the Lighthouse*, *Orlando*, *The Waves*, and *The Years*. The couple also ran the local Hogarth Press, publishing everyone who was anyone, from Freud to Chekhov to Katherine Mansfield. Virginia previously lived for a while at ❹ NO. 46 GORDON SQUARE, just two blocks away, with her sister Vanessa Bell.

Head up Gordon Street to Euston Road, to the ❺ WELLCOME COLLECTION, a real find. The building houses a weird and wonderful array of grisly medical implements and curios once belonging to Sir Henry Wellcome, a pioneering 19th-century pharmacist. Displays include such items as cadaver waxworks, disease-ridden organs, and guillotine blades. The temporary exhibitions are also often memorable, with associated events proving uncanny, especially on the 5th of November, when revellers have been known to celebrate Mexico's Day of the Dead here in macabre style. On an average day, though, the great cafe space (with its spectacular light and ceiling height) and sensational reading room are where smart Londoners come to break away from the British Library – just down the road – when it gets overcrowded.

Another wacky venue can be found hidden in back of Euston Square. Upstairs at ❻ THE MAGIC CIRCLE – home to a museum, theatre, and event space devoted to the magic arts – is a treasure trove of curiosities, including Houdini's handcuffs. The place also boasts the tallest self-supporting spiral staircase in Europe. Back on Euston Road, head west for a block, then turn down Tottenham Court Road and take the first right onto Warren Street, which leads you to Fitzroy Street and onto Fitzroy Square.

Returning to the neighbourhood's historic artistic links, Fitzroy Square (south of Euston Road) is not to be missed. Many famous artists, writers, and statesmen have lived here, with both George Bernard Shaw and (again) Virginia Woolf residing at ❼ NO. 29 at different times.

At the south-east end of the square, follow Fitzroy Street, which morphs into Charlotte Street. The northern section of Charlotte is a mix of 18th-, 19th-, and 20th-century buildings, including the large office block of the advertising agency Saatchi & Saatchi (which has its own pub, named the Pregnant Man, after the firm's first famous ad), whilst the southern half of the street has an enviable reputation for boasting the finest bistros and restaurants. ❽ NAVARRO'S, a family-run tapas eatery, is a personal favourite for being low-key, affordable, and authentic. Here I recommend a quick detour down Scala Street to ❾ POLLOCK'S TOY MUSEUM. The sight of this colourfully painted place, with a Harlequin daubed on the wall next to a first-floor window, always brings a smile to my face. It's a quirky little museum where you can spend an enjoyable half hour exploring the wealth of Victorian toys and dollhouses on display within the dimly lit Dickensian warren of rooms.

Back on Charlotte Street, the nearby ❿ FITZROY TAVERN started out as a coffeehouse in 1883 and became famous during the 1920s to the mid-1950s as a meeting place for artists, intellectuals, and bohemians, including Dylan Thomas and George Orwell. Today,

Opposite: **Pollock's Toy Museum**

the gorgeous ⓫ CHARLOTTE STREET HOTEL just across the street attracts the well-to-do. Come back to where Charlotte meets Rathbone Place in the evening, to the exceptional lounge bar ⓬ BOURNE & HOLLINGSWORTH.

Make your way east along Gresse and Stephen Streets, and cross over Tottenham Court Road to reach Bedford Square. Though now home to Bloomsbury Publishing, publishers of Harry Potter, at No. 30 you'll find a plaque marking the ⓭ FORMER LOCATION OF JONATHAN CAPE, once amongst the leading literary publishers in London, whose titles included T E Lawrence's *The Seven Pillars of Wisdom*, Arthur Ransome's *Swallows and Amazons*, and the first in Ian Fleming's James Bond series, *Casino Royale*. At the south-east corner of the square, take Bloomsbury Street to Great Russell Street. Turn left and then right on Coptic Street.

Never one to conform, Bloomsbury even makes space for a

museum about cartoons a block away from the British Museum! From political sketches to rare original drawings published in *The Beano*, ⑭ THE CARTOON MUSEUM on Little Russell Street, just off Coptic, has everything a comic book lover could ever desire. Continuing on, Museum Street and its environs enjoys a terrific reputation for Korean food as well, so you may want to check out ⑮ BIBIMBAB CAFÉ.

Walking east on Great Russell, I would recommend one last stop before sauntering through the middle of charming Bloomsbury Square Gardens (one of the few squares not associated with a member of the Bloomsbury Group) towards Holborn Station: the ⑯ LONDON REVIEW BOOKSHOP on Bury Place, where you can pick up one of Woolf's books for the ride home.

Above: Fitzroy Square

STARTING POINT
Russell Square Underground Station
GETTING THERE
Piccadilly Line

1 THE HORSE HOSPITAL
Colonnade
London WC1N 1JD
+44 20 7833 3644
www.thehorsehospital.com

2 MCCANN LONDON
7 Herbrand Street, London WC1N 1EX
+44 20 7837 3737
www.mccannlondon.co.uk

3 VIRGINIA & LEONARD
WOOLF'S HOUSE
52 Tavistock Square, London WC1H

4 VIRGINIA WOOLF &
VANESSA BELL'S HOUSE
46 Gordon Square
London WC1H 0PD

5 WELLCOME COLLECTION
183 Euston Road
London NW1 2BE
+44 20 7611 2222
www.wellcomecollection.org

6 THE MAGIC CIRCLE
Centre for the Magic Arts
12 Stephenson Way
London NW1 2HD
+44 20 7387 2222
www.themagiccircle.co.uk

7 GEORGE BERNARD SHAW'S
HOUSE
29 Fitzroy Square
London W1T

8 NAVARRO'S
67 Charlotte Street, London W1T 4PH
+44 20 7637 7713
www.navarros.co.uk

9 POLLOCK'S TOY MUSEUM
1 Scala Street
London W1T 2HL
+44 20 7636 3452
www.pollockstoys.com

10 FITZROY TAVERN
16A Charlotte Street
London W1T 2LY
+44 20 7580 3714

11 CHARLOTTE STREET
HOTEL
15–17 Charlotte Street
London W1T 1RJ
+44 20 7806 2000
www.firmdalehotels.com

12 BOURNE &
HOLLINGSWORTH
28 Rathbone Place
London W1T 1JF
+44 20 7636 8228
www.bourneandhollingsworth.com

13 FORMER LOCATION OF
JONATHAN CAPE
30 Bedford Square
London WC1B 3AA

14 THE CARTOON MUSEUM
35 Little Russell Street
London WC1A 2HH
+44 20 7580 8155
www.cartoonmuseum.org

15 BIBIMBAB CAFÉ
37 Museum Street
London WC1A 1LP
+44 20 7404 8880
www.bibimbabcafe.com

16 LONDON REVIEW
BOOKSHOP
14 Bury Place
London WC1A 2JL
+44 20 7269 9030
www.londonreviewbookshop.co.uk

Opposite: **Bloomsbury Square Gardens**

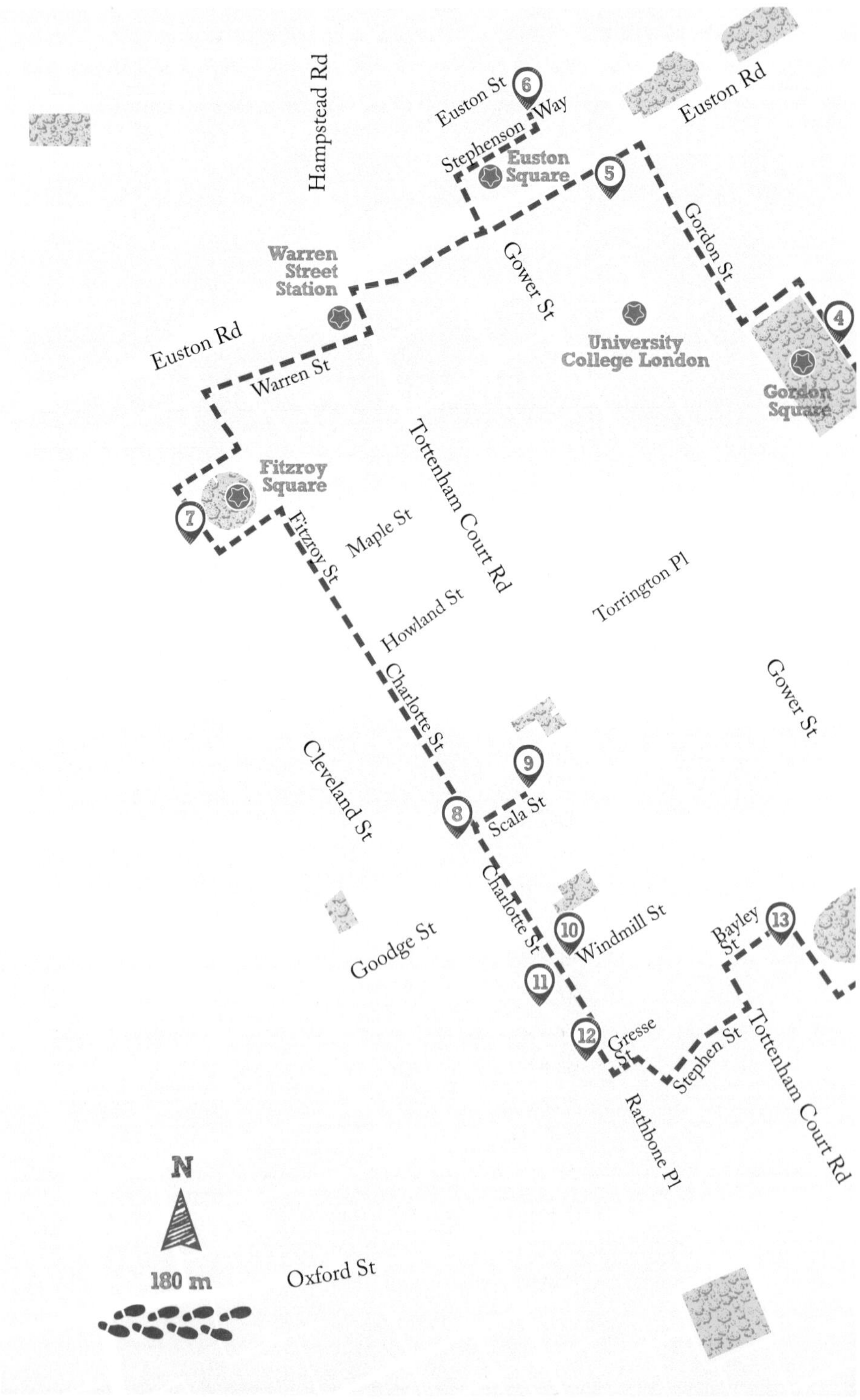

Hampstead Rd
Euston St
6
Stephenson Way
Euston Rd
Euston Square
5
Gordon St
Warren Street Station
Gower St
4
University College London
Gordon Square
Euston Rd
Warren St
Fitzroy Square
7
Fitzroy St
Maple St
Tottenham Court Rd
Torrington Pl
Howland St
Charlotte St
Gower St
Cleveland St
9
8
Scala St
Charlotte St
10
Windmill St
Bayley St
13
Goodge St
11
12
Gresse St
Stephen St
Tottenham Court Rd
Rathbone Pl
N
180 m
Oxford St

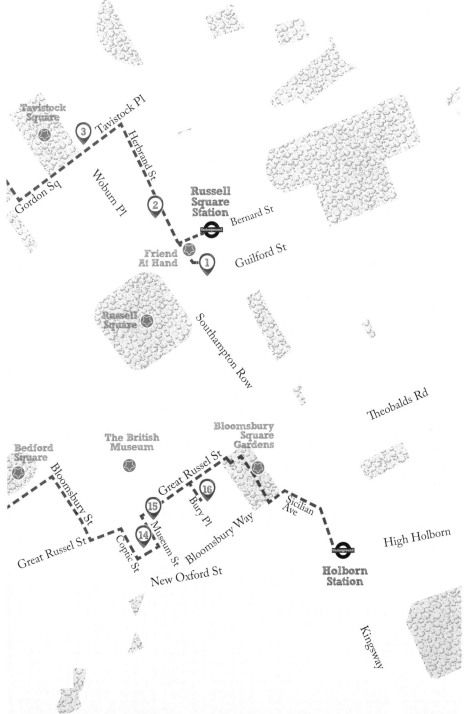

6__ The *Fika* Walk
Marylebone

BEST TIME: Sunday morning
DISTANCE: Approximately 4 kilometres

The Swedish have a term called *fika* which roughly translates as "a break during which people drink coffee, eat some cake or a bun, and chat with their friends," although company is optional. Whether the Swedes adopted Marylebone (pronounced MAR-le-bone) or Marylebone adopted them, is by the by; nowhere in London is *fika* done better. Marylebone has become somewhat of a gastronomic epicentre for London's long-term residents – and businesspeople with large disposable incomes – who fill its restaurants day and night. Here you'll find every conceivable dining experience and cuisine, including French, American, Italian, Mexican, Japanese, and Thai. With the Swedish embassy around the corner and an estimated 60,000 Swedes living in London, it's no wonder *fika* lovers regularly make a beeline to this area.

After shopping on Oxford Street, those who are in the know slip away from the crowds and head down Gee's Court, a tiny alley next to Swedish store H&M across from Bond Street Station, to the hidden piazza at ❶ ST CHRISTOPHER'S PLACE, a stone's throw from Selfridges. *Al fresco* is the buzzword here. Even in winter, people gather at cafe tables outside under patio heating or wander down James Street and other cobblestone side streets in search of a cosy Italian restaurant. It's especially wonderful at Christmastime, when the square and streets are strung with fairy lights, turning the whole place into an enchanted grotto.

Walk north from here, across Wigmore Street to Mandeville Place, and on to the delights of Marylebone, an affluent residential district of terraced Georgian and Edwardian town houses south of Regent's Park. Marylebone still has the feel of a real neighbour-

Opposite: St Christopher's Place

St

Christopher's

Place

Frederick Winsett

RRETT
REET W1
F WESTMINSTER

Clockwise from top left: Daunt Books; Totally Swedish; inside Daunt Books; Swedish Church; Rococo Chocolates; Barret Street sign

hood – rare in central London – attracting a cosmopolitan mix of Europeans, Americans, and Middle Easterners. Residents take a keen interest in local planning issues, keeping a check on the ratio of independent stores to chains on their high street. Marylebone High Street has an eclectic assortment of attractive shops, from haute couture boutiques to specialty food stores, with a distinct cafe culture. Shopping and eating is what Marylebone is all about.

Sundays, locals head for St Vincent Street and Cramer Street Car Park in back of Waitrose for the weekly ❷ MARYLEBONE FARMERS' MARKET. On colder days, you can start off with a hot coffee and a bacon roll from a vendor and wander happily amidst the 30 or 40 outdoor stalls showcasing local produce. The purveyors are delighted to chat and offer tastings, and there is great variety, from oysters to beautiful pastries to wild mushrooms to fresh pasta. Regulars know to turn onto Moxon Street to stock up on high-quality meat at ❸ GINGER PIG, cheeses at ❹ LA FROMAGERIE, or ganache at ❺ ROCOCO CHOCOLATES.

Then it's back to the high-end high street for a spin around the contemporary Scandi-store ❻ SKANDIUM at No. 86, where you can pick up a bag of salty liquorice before heading a few doors down to browse the shelves at legendary London bookstore ❼ DAUNT BOOKS. In many ways, this place is reminiscent of Rizzoli New York: all dark wood panelling, Edwardian fixtures and fittings, and an atrium that filters light throughout the back of the building, all the way from the mezzanine down to the book-filled basement.

Leave behind the eclectic and bustling Marylebone High Street and make your way west on Paddington Street to nearby Chiltern Street, an iconic redbrick stretch of chic boutiques and inviting cafes set amidst Victorian-Gothic architecture.

Head to ❽ THE WALLACE COLLECTION for a dab of culture. At the end of Chiltern Street, make a left onto Blandford and a right onto Manchester Street and the square. The Collection's courtyard restaurant alone is worth the effort, but for admirers of the fine and decorative arts, the works on display in this grand town house on Manchester Square is heaven. With an incredible 25 galleries devoted to 18th-century French paintings and the Old Masters, it's a wonder this place isn't besieged every hour of the day. Perhaps Selfridges, just a block away, draws away the crowds.

Next, foodies and connoisseurs of the finer things know to head for Seymour Place. From Manchester Square, take the Fitzhardinge Street exit to the west and carry on by Portman Square before taking the fourth left onto Seymour Place. At No. 21 you'll find a healthy option at the newly opened ❾ MAE DELI, owned by blogger Ella Woodward, better known simply as Deliciously Ella, or there's the indulgent choice, well-respected Spanish restaurant ❿ DONOSTIA, whose tapas are perfect when you're in a picking mood; be sure to wash them down with their famous Basque cider, which is poured in a rather special way.

All *fika*'d out? Complete a circuit along Seymour Street, and up New Quebec Street to Upper Berkeley. Along the way you'll pass ⓫ THE ZETTER TOWNHOUSE. Inside, you'll find Seymour's Parlour, a drawing-room-style cocktail lounge whose red-painted panelled walls, low lighting, and antique furnishings make for an entertaining detour and glimpse behind the curtain of Marylebone's privileged lifestyle.

Cross Upper Berkeley and continue on along Montagu Street, where things start winding down as you pass by the Swedish embassy before rounding the corner onto Crawford Street. Stop in to the food shop ⓬ TOTALLY SWEDISH and pick up some herring, rye bread, or Löfbergs Lila coffee to take home with you.

From here you can head to Edgware Road Station, join the Nordic contingent at ⓭ THE HARCOURT to enjoy a Swedish cider while cheering on some ice hockey, or pray for the Swedes' cholesterol levels, and your own, at the ⓮ SWEDISH CHURCH on Harcourt Street. The building is easily identifiable by the distinctive Swedish flag – blue with a golden-yellow cross – flapping in the wind outside.

Opposite: Paul Bakery, Marylebone High Street

1 ST CHRISTOPHER'S
PLACE PIAZZA
Marylebone, London W1U
www.stchristophersplace.com/
shops/groom

2 MARYLEBONE
FARMERS' MARKET
Cramer Street Car Park
London W1U

3 GINGER PIG
8–10 Moxon Street
London W1U 4EW
+44 20 7935 7788
www.thegingerpig.co.uk

4 LA FROMAGERIE
2–6 Moxon Street
London W1U 4EW
+44 20 7935 0341
www.lafromagerie.co.uk

5 ROCOCO
CHOCOLATES
3 Moxon Street
London W1U 4EW
+44 20 7935 7780
www.rococochocolates.com

6 SKANDIUM
86 Marylebone High Street
London W1U 4QS
+44 20 7935 2077
www.skandium.com

7 DAUNT BOOKS
83–84 Marylebone High Street
London W1U
+44 20 7224 2295
www.dauntbooks.co.uk

8 THE WALLACE COLLECTION
Hertford House, Manchester Square
London W1U 3BN
+44 20 7563 9500
www.wallacecollection.org

9 THE MAE DELI
21 Seymour Place, London W1H 5BH
www.themaedeli.com

10 DONOSTIA
10 Seymour Place, London W1H 7ND
+44 20 3620 1845
www.donostia.co.uk

11 THE ZETTER
TOWNHOUSE
28–30 Seymour Street
London W1H 7JB
+44 20 7324 4544
www.thezettertownhouse.com

12 TOTALLY SWEDISH
32 Crawford Street, London W1H 1LS
+44 20 7224 9300
www.totallyswedish.com

13 THE HARCOURT
32 Harcourt Street, London W1H 4HX
+44 20 3771 8660
www.theharcourt.com

14 SWEDISH CHURCH
6 Harcourt Street, London W1H 4AG
+44 20 7723 5681
www.swedishchurch.com

Above/Opposite: Totally Swedish's
storefront

Marylebone Rd

Edgware Road Station
Underground

York St

Harcourt St

⑭

⑫

Crawford St

⑬

Chapel St

Crawford St

Old Marylebone Rd

Swedish Embassy

Crawford St

Seymour Pl

Montagu Sq

Edgware Rd

George St

Montagu St

Upper Berkeley St

⑨

⑩

Seymour St

N

120 m

Hyde Park

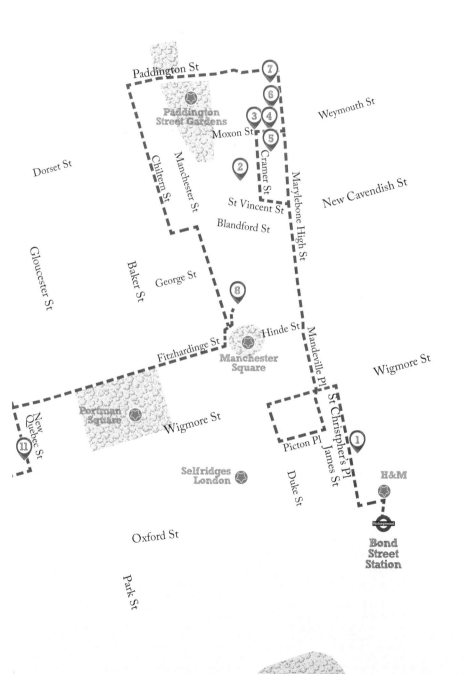

NORTH LONDON ♥

The Rock 'n' Retire Walk

Camden to Primrose Hill

BEST TIME: A clear summer's day, for optimal views

DISTANCE: Approximately 5.5 kilometres

Linked by a picturesque section of the Regent's Canal, Camden Town and neighbouring Primrose Hill could not be more different, with Primrose Hill playing Sunday afternoon to Camden's wild party nights. While Camden is legendary for its open-air markets and live music scene, Primrose Hill is where rock star/model/actor residents go home to recover (Daniel Craig, Jude Law, and Kate Moss have, or have had, crash pads here); lazing on the eponymous hill gazing out over Regent's Park to the south or the cityscape to the east.

Walking on the wackier side first, head down Haverstock Hill towards Chalk Farm Road, which lays claim to a landmark in British music history as well as being the gateway to Camden's interconnecting markets. See that splendid, curved building ahead? A striking blend of Victorian grandeur and industrial-age influence, the ❶ ROUNDHOUSE is a legendary music venue where the likes of Jimi Hendrix, the Doors, Blur, and Oasis have all played. Now an iconic building, it hosted the first major rock 'n' roll event in Camden, in 1966, with Pink Floyd and the Soft Machine performing on the same bill.

Carry on along Chalk Farm Road until you reach the ❷ STABLES MARKET, which is marked by a boundary wall that runs the length of the road. The name stems from the market's previous incarnation as a horse hospital in Victorian times. Whilst there is an accessway adjacent to Morrisons petrol station, I recommend using the market's far grander entrance farther on.

Pause for moment outside ❸ CYBERDOG, easily identifiable by the 5-metre-high male and female cyborgs on either side of the

Opposite: Entrance to Cyberdog, Stables Market

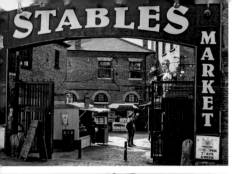

Clockwise from top left: Camden Stables Market – main entrance, food stall inside the market, more stalls; street food along Regent's Canal; Camden Lock; Camden Lock sign

doorway. Inside this clothes shop, it's more like a rave than a retail outlet; complete with UV-lit backdrop and live dancers performing around poles at all times of day. This place is a Camden rite of passage.

Once you're inside the heart of the market, your senses will go into overdrive with the wonderful smells of Asian street food frying along the main strip, where vendors have created a slice of Thailand/Korea. As you navigate through a hive of narrow corridors, you can also expect to see plenty of bustiers, velvet, and leather on sale where stalls and shops offer a crazy fusion of decades and trends – places like ❶ COLLECTIF, which offers a blend of fifties fashion with a smattering of Japanese street style, and ❺ BURLESKA CORSETS, for the glamour-goth/burlesque set. The idiosyncratic touches that are dotted all around, like cast- and wrought-iron statues of horses and equestrian reliefs, are what really set this place apart, though.

Keep a lookout for the entrance to ❻ HORSE TUNNEL MARKET, recognizable by the large carved steeds guarding its entrance. Hidden beneath the famous venue are what are known as the Camden Catacombs, an extensive web of vaults and underground passageways that originally provided stabling, storage, and tack space for scores of pit ponies serving the railway/canal interchange situated above. It is possible to glimpse a small portion of the network via the restored canal-side buildings along the Lock, which you'll pass later in the walk.

Crossing Camden Lock Place, you'll enter a newer phase of development, ❼ CAMDEN LOCK MARKET, where the shops are more about home decorations, jewellery, and accessories. Here the vibe of the market mellows out into a chilled breakout area where visitors and buskers gather around Regent's Canal. It's all about finding a place to sit down in the sunshine with a tasty bite of street food, as you people-watch to your heart's content.

Before strolling along the canal path to Primrose Hill, take a side trip down Camden High Street. For fans of live music, this neck of the woods is worth a return visit one evening to enjoy a full spectrum of offerings, from hard rock to the blues, packing in more performance spaces per square mile than practically anywhere else in London Town. First up is the ⑧ ELECTRIC BALLROOM. By night, this is one of the city's most renowned music and performance venues, but come Sunday, it takes a day off from rock 'n' roll to host a lively indoor market. Around the corner, at Parkway, the ⑨ JAZZ CAFE and ⑩ GREEN NOTE are among the local favourites.

Have a wander down Parkway and you'll also pass Albert Street, where the Jewish Museum is located. Turn up Gloucester Avenue and follow the road around to the sweeping group of terraced Italianate villas on Gloucester Crescent, where the playwright Alan Bennett lived for many years. Turn right on Oval Road and cross over the canal to ⑪ GILBEY'S YARD and its restored canal buildings.

When you're ready to get away from the noise and crowds, and experience the flipside, head down the steps alongside the flamboyant ⑫ PIRATE CASTLE to the canal path, nestled in amongst the industrial warehouses next to Camden Lock. Built in 1977, the building looks like some kind of folly, with medieval castle turrets – a jolly setting for a children's water sports centre. This next stretch of walkway along the canal feels like entering a parallel universe. Residents of the beautiful Victorian terraced houses keep their backyards shipshape for the viewing public with wooden decking, tidy landscaping, and bounteous flowering pots. Stick to the canal path until you round the bend at Cumberland Basin. You'll know you've arrived when you see the giant floating Chinese restaurant, Feng Shang Princess, an odd but flashy and fun holdover from Camden.

Come off at Broad Walk and turn left onto St Mark's Square which leads to Primrose Hill Park. This is where North Londoners come to graze. Once the sun emerges, it's time to play, as people of all ages spread out their blankets on the grass, pop open the fizz, and chat animatedly with friends.

Head up to the ⑬ SUMMIT OF PRIMROSE HILL – crossing the park diagonally – and enjoy the gorgeous view of the city before heading straight back down to Regent's Park Road and into the heart of the district. Sidle up to the bar at ⑭ THE QUEENS, grab a table

Above: Pirate Castle; Below: Camden Lock

The pastel town houses of Chalcott Square

at a sidewalk cafe, or settle into a garden courtyard in back of one of the many neighbourhood pubs. For indoor dining, ⑨ LEMONIA is a local favourite, so I advise you to reserve a table ahead of time as it is often booked up on summer days. Explore the high street's boutiques and shops, chief among them local independent bookshop ⑩ PRIMROSE HILL BOOKS.

From here, cut down Berkley Road and enjoy a mellow stroll around Chalcot Square, with its splendid pastel-coloured houses, then follow Chalcot Road to the corner of Fitzroy Road and turn left. Here is where you're most likely to encounter summer revellers, outside the Princess of Wales and Landowne public houses, or drifting down from the Pembroke at the top of Gloucester Avenue. Turn right after the Pembroke and cross the railway bridge at the top of Regent's Park Road. Continue straight on Bridge Approach and then take a right on Adelaide Road to return to Chalk Farm Station, from where you set out.

Primrose Hill Village, Regent's Park Road

Chalk Farm Underground Station
Northern Line

Chalk Farm Road
London NW1 8EH
+44 300 678 9222
www.roundhouse.org.uk

Chalk Farm Road
London NW1 8AH
+44 20 7485 5511
www.camdenmarket.com

Stables Market, Chalk Farm Road
London NW1 8AH
+44 20 7482 2842
www.cyberdog.net

Unit 036, The Stables Market
Chalk Farm Road
London NW1 8AH
www.camdenmarket.com/shops/
collectif

Unit 10B, The Stables Market
Chalk Farm Road
London NW1 8AH
+44 20 7485 3120
www.burleska.co.uk/camden-shop

The Stables Market
Chalk Farm Road
London NW1 8AH

56 Camden Lock Place
London NW1 8AF

184 Camden High Street
London NW1 8QP
+44 20 7485 9006
www.electricballroom.co.uk

5 Parkway
London NW1 7PG
+44 20 7485 6834
www.thejazzcafelondon.com

106 Parkway, London NW1 7AN
+44 20 7485 9899
www.greennote.co.uk

(Entrance to Old Horse Tunnels)
London NW1 8HB

Oval Road, London NW1 7EA
+44 20 7267 6605
www.thepiratecastle.org

Primrose Hill Park, London NW3 3AX

49 Regent's Park Road
London NW1 8XD
+44 020 7586 0408
www.thequeensprimrosehill.co.uk

134 Regent's Park Road
London NW1 8XL
+44 20 7586 2022
www.primrosehillbooks.com

89 Regent's Park Road
London NW1 8UY
+44 20 7586 7454
www.lemonia.co.uk

Opposite: **View of the city from Primrose Hill**

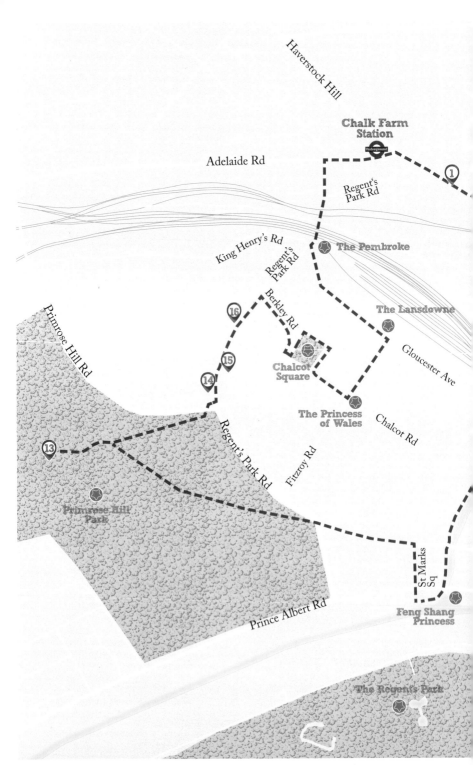

Ferdinand St

Kentish Town Rd

Chalk Farm Rd

Morrisons
Petrol
Station

③

②
④
⑤

⑥
⑦

Castlehaven Rd

⑪

Gilbeys Yard

⑫

Jamestown Rd

Camden High St

⑧

Kentish Town Rd

Gloucester Cres

Oval Rd

⑨

Regent's Canal

Regent's Park Rd

Parkway

⑩

Jewish Museum

Camden High St

Delancey St

N

120 m

The Vintage Walk

Islington to Barnsbury to Exmouth Market

BEST TIME: Sunday 10am–2pm, for the farmer's market;
or Monday–Friday 9am–noon, before the lunch rush at
Exmouth Market
DISTANCE: Approximately 6 kilometres

For me, Islington is my Brighton-Without-the-Sea. It's where I go
when I'm missing the vintage and second-hand stores of Brighton's
North Laine; its warren of streets, the period houses set around
garden squares, the fringe comedy and music scene, the vibe.

From Angel Station I always head to ❶ CAMDEN PASSAGE
first. Outside the station, move along the covered pedestrian walkway ahead, down the steps past The York pub and cross straight
over Duncan Street. Host to an antiques market on Wednesdays
and Saturdays, Camden Passage is among my favourite places to
potter around. I recommend starting out with brunch at ❷ THE
BREAKFAST CLUB, whose decor pays homage to the American
director John Hughes and the eighties. Just opposite is ❸ ANNIE'S,
where you can rifle through racks of flapper dressers and beaded
gowns, some garments dating as far back as the forties and even the
twenties. Dare to venture inside ❹ AQUAMARINE ANTIQUES,
down Pierrepoint Row, for its baffling combination of stuffed animals
and military memorabilia. The lane grows narrower as you stroll past
the Camden Head pub and the side entrance that leads up to ❺
ANGEL COMEDY, whose fringe performances make for one of
the funniest nights out in London.

Then it's up Essex Road for some go-to vintage and vinyl stores. The
1940s-to-1970s vibe at ❻ PAST CARING is perfect for picking up
a mid-century typewriter. Record lovers head for ❼ FLASHBACK
RECORDS. Once you've had your fill of yesteryear, cut over on

Opposite: Camden Passage

Antiques
&
Collectable

Clockwise from top left: Shop window, Camden Passage; The Breakfast Club; building detail on Islington High Street; Camden Passage street sign; decorative window along Camden Passage

Cross Street, and continue past Upper Street to Almeida Street, home to the renowned ❸ ALMEIDA THEATRE.

The first time I wandered beyond the theatre to Milner Square, I was impressed by the distinctive neoclassical houses. I later learnt that these were designed by Roumieu and Gough, who also designed the Islington Literary and Philosophical Institute (now the Almeida Theatre) in 1837. Exiting the square to the north, follow Milner Place to Barnsbury Street and take a left. Moving into the Barnsbury conservation area, turn left on Thornhill Road. Here you'll find ❾ THE ALBION public house, winner of the Observer Food Monthly award for "Best Sunday Lunch 2009" and one of the *Independent*'s "Top 50 Sunday Lunch Venues." A Georgian gem with a wisteria-covered façade and log-fire ambience, it even boasts a picturesque walled garden.

Past the Albion, turn east on Richmond Avenue and make your way around the splendid Georgian plaza Gibson Square to the end of "gastronomical" Theberton Street, where French bistro ❿ LE SACRE COEUR vies for customers alongside Middle Eastern restaurants ⓫ MEM & LAZ BRASSERIE and ⓬ KILIS KITCHEN, and several other family-run eateries. As with Brighton, the restaurateurs along this short strip value ambience as much as they do good food. Be sure to check out some of the interiors.

Turn right at the end of Theberton Street onto Upper Street and you're back at Islington Green and ⓭ EVERYMAN SCREEN ON THE GREEN, a great little retro picture house diagonally across the green from Camden Passage.

For a true locals' experience, come Sunday mornings (between 10am and 2pm) residents know to head for ⓮ ISLINGTON FARMERS' MARKET on Chapel Market. Take a shortcut from Upper Street, turning right into the pedestrian passageway between the clothing shops Accessorize and Oasis and then left on Liverpool Street and right on Chapel Market. Located between Baron and Penton Streets, this was London's first farmers' market and has become its most established. Despite being surrounded by major stores and a shopping centre, the market holds its own, retaining its unpretentious character.

Leaving Islington behind, turn left down Penton Street (by the Joker bar); you're heading to ⑮ EXMOUTH MARKET on the Finsbury/Clerkenwell borders. Along the way, you'll pass through Claremont Square, which was developed between 1821 and 1828 and still has its original 19th-century railings; Myddleton Square Gardens, which has been a public green for almost 200 years; and Wilmington Square. Here, there is a pedestrian walkway instead of a road along the north side, a late-19th-century pavilion and drinking fountain, numerous trees and conifers, roses, and ornamental elements.

Two blocks on from Wilmington Square and you arrive at Exmouth Market. I love the energy of this street. Even though you're in the centre of city, it feels more like the edgy seaside town of Brighton. This was all a run-down area of old warehouses and factories, until the publishing, design, and architecture firms moved in. Today, it is one of East London's most desirable addresses.

There's a variety of stylish independent shops and restaurants lining the pedestrianized street. Starting out, you'll pass local favourite the ⑯ EXMOUTH ARMS, a pub that appeals to both hipsters and traditionalists. Coffee lovers make a beeline for ⑰ CARAVAN, right around the corner, where they can gaze out onto the market from the cafe's big windows. ⑱ MORO (Iberian-with-a-North-African-twist Mediterranean fare) regularly appears on London's top restaurant lists and their customers spill out into their sibling tapas bar next door, Morito.

Monday to Friday, the street food merchants set up their stalls from mid-morning, with city workers strolling into the leafy square at lunchtime to sample cuisines from all over the culinary map: Ghana, Mexico, Bangladesh, Spain, and more. In the warmer months, patrons wander down Northampton Row, or Spa Fields Lane, to Spa Fields Park, a favoured retreat tucked alongside a 240-year-old chapel. With its assortment of public benches and secluded alcoves, this is a perfect spot for lunch.

Above & Below: **Exmouth Market**

Around the corner on Rosebery Avenue, ⑲ OLD FINSBURY TOWN HALL is one of London's hidden treasures. This fusion of Regency and Victorian architecture exudes opulence and glamour with splashes of Art Nouveau décor. Several times a year, the venue is also the location of Clerkenwell Vintage Fashion Fair, where international fashionistas and lovers of retro fashion come in droves to source apparel from the crinoline-wearing 1800s all the way up through the power-dressing heydays of the 1980s. As an extra flourish, there's even the pop-up Tea Room des Artistes, where you can sample a quintessential English tea, served in fine vintage china cups along with a classic Victoria sponge cake.

Above: The Old Red Lion Theatre and Pub

From here, you can make you way back to Angel Station, continuing along Rosebery Avenue past Sadler's Wells Theatre, London's leading venue for international dance. Take a left onto St John's and you'll come across the ⑳ OLD RED LION THEATRE, which not only puts on some great productions but is officially the favourite pub of *Trainspotting* author Irvine Welsh whenever he is in London, and is popular with actors and drama students (Ray Winstone is known to pop in). If you get a second wind, you can stay on and sample a play, comedy performance, music gig, or ballet, or simply cross over Pentonville Road to Angel, and head back home with your vintage goodie bags and happy memories.

Opposite: Finsbury Town Hall

STARTING POINT
Angel Underground Station

GETTING THERE
Northern Line

1 CAMDEN PASSAGE
Islington, London N1 8EA

2 THE BREAKFAST CLUB
31 Camden Passage, London N1 8EA
+44 20 7226 5454
www.thebreakfastclubcafes.com

3 ANNIE'S
12 Camden Passage, London N1 8ED
+44 20 7359 0796
www.anniesvintageclothing.co.uk

4 AQUAMARINE
ANTIQUES
14 Pierrepoint Row, London N1 8EF
+44 20 7359 0197

5 ANGEL COMEDY
2 Camden Passage, London N1 8DY
+44 7500 104816
www.angelcomedy.co.uk

6 PAST CARING
54 Essex Road, London N1

7 FLASHBACK RECORDS
50 Essex Road, London N1 8LR
+44 20 7354 9356
www.flashback.co.uk

8 ALMEIDA THEATRE
Almeida Street, London N1 1TA
+44 20 7359 4404
www.almeida.co.uk

9 THE ALBION
10 Thornhill Road, London N1 1HW
+44 20 7607 7450
www.the-albion.co.uk

10 LE SACRE COEUR
18 Theberton Street, London N1 0QX
+44 20 7354 2618
www.lesacrecoeurbistro.co.uk

11 MEM & LAZ BRASSERIE
8 Theberton Street, London N1 0QX
+44 20 7704 9089
www.memlaz.co.uk

12 KILIS KITCHEN
4 Theberton Street, London N1 0QX
+44 20 7226 5489
www.kilis.co.uk

13 EVERYMAN SCREEN
ON THE GREEN
83 Upper Street, London N1 0NP
+44 871 906 9060
www.everymancinema.com

14 ISLINGTON FARMERS'
MARKET
Chapel Market, Penton Street
London N1 9PZ

15 EXMOUTH MARKET
Clerkenwell, London EC1R 4QL
www.exmouth.london

16 EXMOUTH ARMS
23 Exmouth Market
London EC1R 4QL
+44 20 3551 4772
www.exmoutharms.com

17 CARAVAN
11–13 Exmouth Market
London EC1R 4QD
+44 20 7833 8115
www.caravanonexmouth.co.uk

18 MORO
34–36 Exmouth Market
London EC1R 4QE
+44 20 7833 8336
www.moro.co.uk

19 OLD FINSBURY TOWN HALL
Rosebery Avenue
London EC1R 4RP
+44 20 7713 7710
www.theoldfinsburytownhall.co.uk

20 OLD RED LION THEATRE
418 St John Street, London EC1V 4NJ
+44 20 7837 7816
www.oldredliontheatre.co.uk

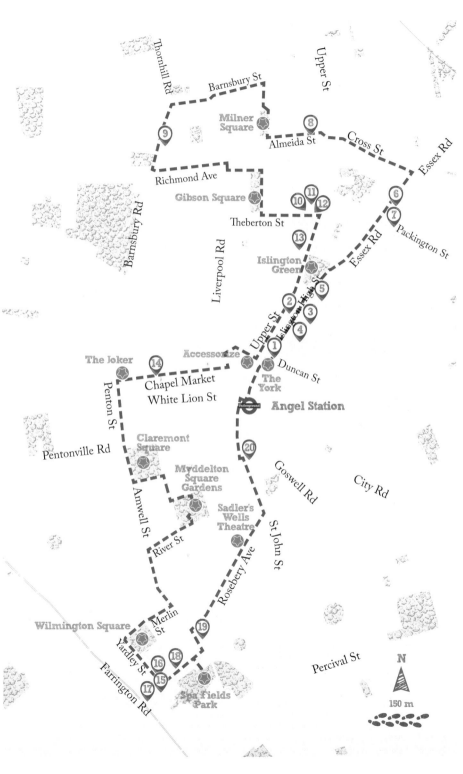

9__ The Walk With the Most Views

Alexandra Palace to Muswell Hill to Highgate Wood

BEST TIME: Spring or autumn
DISTANCE: Approximately 6 kilometres

No place in North London tops ➊ ALEXANDRA PALACE for far-reaching panoramic views. Set within 196 acres of parkland, resting on a hilltop, the palace opened on 24 May 1873, Queen Victoria's birthday, and was visited by 120,000 people in the first two weeks. Built at a time when Britain was leading the Industrial Revolution and wanted to let the world know, the site gained a reputation as the People's Palace. No kings or queens have ever lived here.

Though there are several approaches to Ally Pally (as it is fondly known), it's best to start from Alexandra Palace BR Station rather than Wood Green. Enter Alexandra Park at South Terrace, and take the left fork to wend your way along one of the many footpaths, heading south west.

The ascent is exhilarating, with some parts wooded and other sections opening into wide, grassy plateaus. Landscaped for recreational use during the Victorian era, much entertainment was put on here back in the day, when the park even featured a bandstand and a racecourse. Survey the layout of the urban planning below, and you can see the curvature of the old track, which was still operating as recently as 1970.

"But what of the palace?" you may well be wondering. For the longest time during your walk, you'll find it obscured from view, and then – through a break in the trees – there it is, in all its formal 19th-century grandeur; a showcase for Victorian pomp and

Opposite: View from Alexandra Palace

Clockwise from top left: The Boating Lake, Alexandra Park; detail of lamps in front of Alexandra Palace; walking path, Alexandra Park; view from Muswell Hill; Alexandra Palace

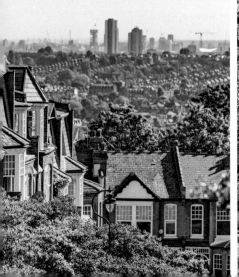

ceremony. Cut through the gap and rejoin the path bearing left and up to the palace.

Influenced somewhat by railway architecture of the time, this elegant building rises up from its hilltop locale with soaring atrium ceilings supported by ornamental columns, and stunning rose windows – not to neglect its glorious wraparound promenade. From here, looking out over the city, you can see London's northern terraces cascading across ancient ridges. In the distance, the silhouette of the Shard, the capital's highest skyscraper (95 storeys), appears no bigger than the inch gap between your thumb and forefinger, whilst the dome of St Paul's is no larger than a beetle's husk.

The BBC began transmitting the news from Ally Pally in 1935, the voice of the famed Edith Cowell broadcasting into all those houses you see below and throughout the country. These BBC programs are woven into the fabric of the lives of generations of Britons, with the 1950s proving particularly memorable, as the studios became home to the greats of British children's television, including Andy Pandy and Muffin the Mule. Nowadays, people travel here from far and wide for concerts and conventions, whilst families make their way over to the popular ice rink, with its dramatic backdrop of original Victorian architecture. Behind the palace, you'll find the ❷ BOATING LAKE, where generations of North Londoners have clambered aboard the pedalos for an hour's entertainment. There's also the ❸ LAKESIDE CAFÉ, where you can stop off for refreshments.

As far back as the 12th century, nearby Muswell Hill has been a village and, whilst it has grown considerably in size over time, it has retained an air of seclusion, in part because it is not connected to a rail network and is at too high an elevation for underground services. It also commands extensive views. To reach its shops and cafes, head back to the front of the palace and turn right down the driveway until you come to the first footpath by the small car park. Head along the path, veering left where the path forks, and after 200 metres you'll pass the Grove Café. This is your half way mark. Keep following the path around, as it bears right, and you'll reach the park exit. At the main road, head up to the roundabout. The many residential thoroughfares which radiate from the fine central business quarter are known as the Exchange. There are eateries and stores aplenty, and one place not to be missed is ❹ W MARTYN, a coffee and provision shop on Muswell Hill Broadway, which has been trading since 1897.

Turn onto Queen's Avenue, leading off the Exchange, and you are transported back in time to an Edwardian suburb. Laid out in curving lines, the houses draw on elements of vernacular architecture, with cat-slide gables and façades of hung tiles. This period of the Arts and Crafts movement led to what is known as Queen Anne or Domestic Revival-style architecture, when the fussy elements of Victorian buildings began to disappear. Muswell Hill came under the influence of these then modern designs, inspired by men like Norman Shaw and C F A Voysey. The commodious terraced houses attracted middle-class residents, mostly bankers, with many large family homes built, each distinct from its neighbour.

Make a left turn on Fortis Green Road, and at the end of Fortis Green, cross over to St James's Lane. Just before the archway, head up the steps opposite Autowerke (a garage workshop), where you'll find a shortcut to Highgate Wood via a section of ❺ PARKLAND WALK.

The Parkland Walk follows an overgrown path, which was once the old rail line. Urban myths have it that trains can be heard rumbling along the route close to the Highgate tunnels, even though the track was removed long ago, and that the whole area has been cursed by gypsies who were evicted from the pre-Alexandra Palace site.

The path breaks off at Cranley Gardens, where you can wander through the gates to a 70-acre ancient woodland. Life-long locals can still remember excavation digs in the 1970s where evidence of a Roman settlement was established here. In medieval times, the woods were the hunting estate of the Bishop of London. Today, it is both a conservation area and a public space.

Opposite: Highgate Wood

On entering Highgate Wood, keep to the path straight ahead, passing Keeper's Cottage. Evergreen holly trees are to be found everywhere, as well as hornbeams and solid oaks. Pass Bridge Gate and follow the curve of the asphalt path all the way around to the recreational ground. Along the way you may notice several fenced conservation areas. These are cordoned off periodically so the woodland's vegetation has the chance to regenerate. At the edges of a large clearing, home to the sports ground, you'll find the ⑥ PAVILION CAFE, with an enclosed area of outdoor terraced seating, creating a winning ambience.

Across the road is Queens Wood, a less-tame forest popular for walking dogs; save this for another day and conclude the walk here, simply by joining the path on the far side of the cafe and walking parallel to the football pitches. Keep following the bend around, leaving the clearing behind, until you reach Gypsy Gate. Here, turn right on Muswell Hill Road where you'll find access to Highgate Station either via the steep steps on Wood Lane or at grade level on Archway Road. Those with extra endurance can continue on along the Parkland Walk, which resumes here, for a full day of outdoor exploration among London's florae and fauna.

STARTING POINT
Alexandra Palace BR Station

GETTING THERE
Overground from Moorgate
or King's Cross

① ALEXANDRA PALACE
Alexandra Palace Way
London N22 7AY
+44 20 8365 2121
www.alexandrapalace.com

② BOATING LAKE
Alexandra Palace Way, London N22

③ LAKESIDE CAFÉ
Alexandra Palace Way, London N22
www.lakesidecafe.co.uk

④ W MARTYN
135 Muswell Hill Broadway
London N10 3RS
+44 20 8883 5642
www.wmartyn.co.uk

⑤ PARKLAND WALK
Muswell Hill, London N10

⑥ PAVILION CAFE
Highgate Wood
Muswell Hill Road, London N10 3JN
+44 20 8444 4777

Opposite: Pavilion Cafe in Highgate Wood

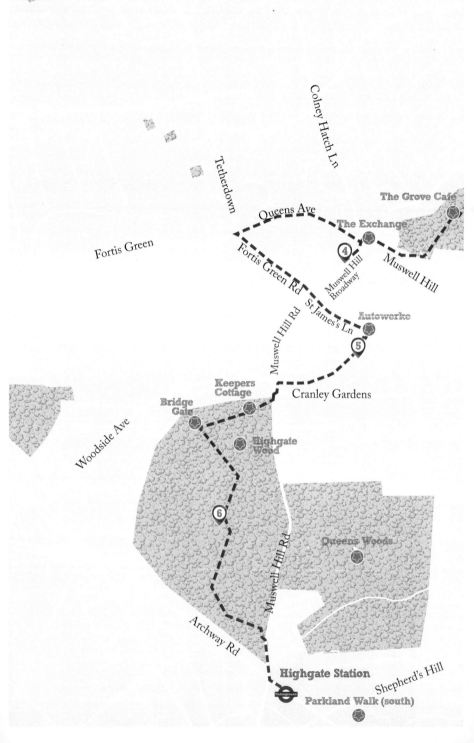

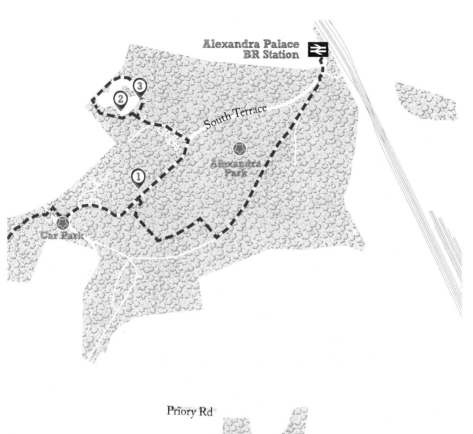

Alexandra Palace
BR Station

South Terrace

Alexandra
Park

① ② ③

Car Park

Priory Rd

Park Rd

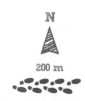

N

200 m

10__ The Heath Walk

Hampstead Heath

BEST TIME: A clear day, any season
DISTANCE: Approximately 5 kilometres

Four miles from central London, Hampstead Heath is a large, ancient park spread over 800 acres. Records of its existence date back to the Middle Ages and it survives today as an island of countryside, accessible to all, thanks to a determined band of Victorian campaigners who saved it from development. The first time I visited here, I was thoroughly daunted by the prospect of venturing too far off the beaten track, perhaps because I had only ever known the landscaped parks and flat commons of South and West London. I made it as far as the Mixed Bathing Pond, 100 metres past the entrance, and settled on the grass by the water with some friends amidst the vibrant company of neighbourhood locals. Years later, I climbed up Parliament Hill onto the Heath, where I could at last get the lay of the land and gain my bearings. So, that's where I'm steering you first.

Setting off from Hampstead Heath BR Station, it's a straightforward march up to ❶ PARLIAMENT HILL, the gateway to the Heath, which serves up a stunning 360-degree view of London, as well as glorious sunrises and sunsets. Follow the path up the steep incline. When the weather is good, you'll find yourself surrounded by people flying kites of all descriptions. Myth has it that the world's most notorious pyromaniac suggested friends gather here, on Parliament Hill, one cold autumn eve to witness his greatest display. The year was 1605, the day was November the 5th, and the ringleader was Guy Fawkes. Whilst they didn't get their fireworks that night, residents today turn out in force to enjoy the New Year and Bonfire Night pyrotechnics.

Opposite: View of the city from Parliament Hill

Above: Kenwood House; Below: Kenwood Ladies' Bathing Pond

Upon reaching the summit, you'll be rewarded with the spectacular panoramic cityscape to the south, bringing into sharp focus landmarks such as the Shard, the Gherkin, and Westminster, with the sunlight shimmering off their glasswork. But it's the views across the Heath to the east and north that will restore your equilibrium. Marvellously, you'll feel closer to "Constable Country" than a metropolis, imagining the sounds of a horse-drawn cart coming over the crest of the hill or picturing a pastoral scene with the landscape blanketed white with snow. Far from any road, no roar of traffic will reach your ears, and the view to the northeast is of a church steeple rising from the hamlet of Highgate, which borders the Heath. Only a single tower block, way in the distance, alludes to modern life.

Walk down Parliament Hill to the ponds; bear left and the first pond you'll pass on your right is called Highgate No. 1, followed by Highgate Men's Bathing Pond and the Model Boating Pond. The park exit to the right of Highgate No. 1 leads to Swain's Lane and on to Highgate Cemetery, but you're heading on to the footpath just past the Model Boating Pond, where you'll see a stream of people coming and going from the Heath. Walk their way and join the lane that runs the park's perimeter, turning north. This is Millfield Lane, which leads to ❹ KENWOOD HOUSE. A fine 18th-century country home re-modelled by Robert Adam between 1764 and 1779, it contains an impressive art collection, including works by Rembrandt, Vermeer, Turner, Gainsborough, and Reynolds.

En route, the women among you might like to explore the famed ❷ KENWOOD LADIES' BATHING POND, officially opened in 1925. Where the path to the pond starts, you'll see a "Women Only" sign. Follow it, and you'll enter a meadow; beyond which is the swimming area. Rumour has it that the Hollywood movie star Katharine Hepburn showed up once for a candlelit swim under the cover of night. I like to imagine women of all ages, creeds, and classes congregating here over the decades. What would it have been like to wade and swim alongside fellow bathers in the 1960s and '70s? How different would it have been in the '50s? Whilst we

leave these hardy specimens braving the cold lake waters, let's make for Kenwood.

Resume your walk along Millfield Lane, with its iron railing to your left and residential houses on your right, and after about 800 metres you'll come out into a clearing. As the hill rises, follow the boundary fence on the left until you reach Millfield Gate and enter the estate of Kenwood House. Some of you may recognize the scene ahead from films such as *Notting Hill* and *Belle*. The grounds also include an impressive ❸ OPEN-AIR THEATRE, where audiences flock in the summer months for music concerts in the heat of the day or beneath the stars after nightfall.

A half-moon lawn in front of the house sets off its elegant frontage to perfection. You can wander a series of meandering paths, designed by a celebrated Georgian landscape gardener, around the property. Locals rave about the light and dark pink blooms of the rhododendrons, come spring. Many visitors trot up to the renowned

stately home simply to enjoy the ❺ BREW HOUSE cafe, with its rustic interior and leafy garden terrace beyond.

Follow the main path around to the right; it's time to dive into the Heath's dense forest. Entering the woods, keep to the straight path. After about half a kilometre, you'll come out into a clearing. In the distance ahead of you is Parliament Hill and 500 metres across the field to your left are the ponds you passed earlier on. At the end of the path you're on, turn right, zigzagging along the short series of trails through the woods to the Mixed Bathing Pond (if in doubt, simply ask). Cross the bridge between the Mixed Bathing Pond and the Hampstead No. 2 Pond. On the other side, bear left and exit the park onto South End Road. Note the parade of shops across the street. Turn left and you'll find yourself back at the train station where you began your tour of the Heath.

Above: Pond by the open-air theatre

STARTING POINT
Hampstead Heath BR Station

GETTING THERE
Overground on Richmond
to Stratford Line

1 KENWOOD PARLIAMENT
HILL
Hampstead Heath,
London NW3 1TH

2 LADIES' BATHING POND
Hampstead Heath,
London NW5 1QR

3 KENWOOD OPEN-AIR
THEATRE
Hampstead Heath, London NW3 7JR
+44 370 333 1181
www.english-heritage.org.uk

4 KENWOOD HOUSE
Hampstead Lane, London NW3 7JR
+44 370 333 1181
www.english-heritage.org.uk

5 BREW HOUSE
Kenwood House, Hampstead Lane
London NW3 7JR
+44 20 8348 4073

Below: Hampstead Heath bathing pond

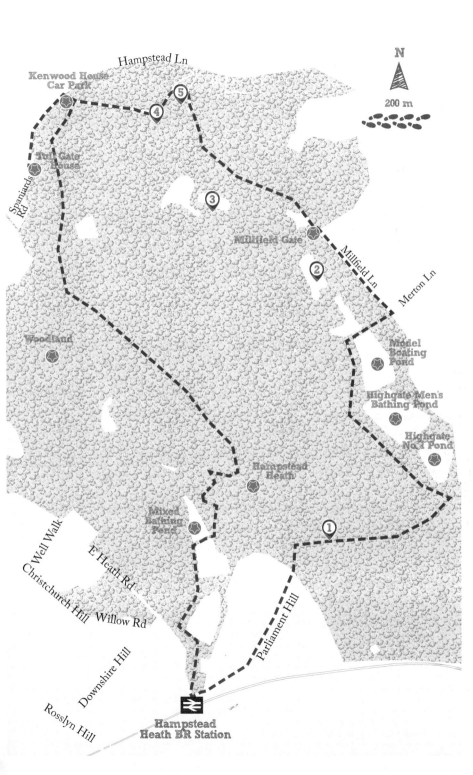

11 ___ The Victorian Valhalla Walk

Highgate

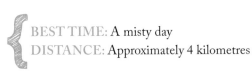

BEST TIME: A misty day
DISTANCE: Approximately 4 kilometres

This expedition takes in the pleasing and atmospheric village of Highgate and culminates in the Victorian Valhalla that is its centrepiece: Highgate Cemetery, the burial place of a multitude of peerless men (and a few memorable women) during Queen Victoria's reign.

You must be made of stern stuff to make the nearly mile-long ascent along Southwood Lane – a steep hill that connects Highgate Station to the village. Whilst planning this walk for a sunny spring or summer morning may seem more sensible, my peculiar recommendation is to choose a dreary, grey day – drizzly even. Better still, a foggy one, when you can barely see a few yards ahead. Perhaps it is the disadvantage of being on such a severe incline, or the claustrophobic feeling of the high walls closing in on you, or how the narrow house, with its high foundations, towers overhead at the junction of Jackson's and Southwood Lanes, but it all adds to the eeriness factor. The first time I made my way up here, the hairs on the back of my neck stood up, an effect that is absent in glorious sunshine. For this outing, you'll want to be feeling Dickensian in mood. Fittingly, Dickens's entire family had lodgings nearby, and the family crypt is located in Highgate Cemetery.

At the top of the lane is Highgate High Street, the hub of village life. Save window-shopping and restaurant browsing for some other time; instead turn right, towards the roundabout, and left on Highgate West Hill (known simply as West Hill), for a history lesson of sorts. The story goes that in 1837, not long after her coronation,

Opposite: Statuary in Highgate Cemetery

Clockwise from top left: Highgate Cemetery;
modern glass house on Swain's Lane; Karl
Marx's grave; overgrown tombstones in
Highgate Cemetery; Lauderdale House

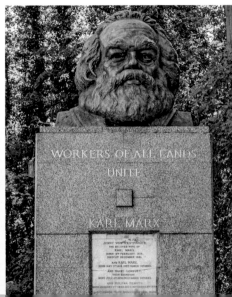

a young Queen Victoria was riding down West Hill in a carriage, when the horses bolted. The landlord of the nearby Fox and Crown (no longer there), seeing the out-of-control coach careening down the hill, rushed out and managed to halt it, narrowly averting disaster. Had he not been there, Victoria might have been killed – and the Victorian era wiped from the slate of history.

At the junction that connects West Hill to the Grove and South Grove, you'll pass ❶ THE FLASK public house. William Hogarth is said to have patronized the establishment, and rumours abound that a ghost in a cavalier costume haunts the place, wandering through the main bar and disappearing into a wall. Another tale goes that legendary highwayman Dick Turpin hid here on one occasion. Ten years ago, you were more likely to see English comedian Eric Idle propping up the bar with his good friend David Attenborough. Two hundred years ago, English poet and philosopher Samuel Taylor Coleridge lived nearby, at ❷ NO. 3 THE GROVE, where he welcomed a steady stream of eminent Georgian visitors, including Dante Gabriel Rossetti and John Stuart Mill.

Around the corner, in back of the Flask, walk up South Grove to the dignified-looking Pond Square. No. 11 South Grove is home to the ❸ HIGHGATE LITERARY AND SCIENTIFIC INSTITUTION, founded in 1839 "for the promotion of useful and scientific knowledge." Swain's Lane leads off the square, easily sought out thanks to the radio mast towering behind the institute. This is the most atmospheric approach to ❹ HIGHGATE CEMETERY.

Whilst the incline here is steep, mercifully, you're heading downhill. After about 200 metres you'll walk by a very modern-looking glass residence (privately owned); continue another 200 metres until you pass Waterlow Park, on your left. Not far to go now. The entrance to the cemetery will be recognizable by ivy-clad railings to one side and a stone-turreted lodge on the other. After it opened in 1839, Highgate Cemetery became the most fashionable Victorian necropolis in London. Imagine the great pomp and ceremony of a burial back then, with mourners in their finery gathered together as the hearse was driven up. Again, I urge you to go on the most austere of days – rain, snow, fog – the bleaker, the better.

To fully mine the history of this burial ground and what it stands for, one must appreciate how fertile a period England's Victorian era was, brimming with new ideas in religion, politics, and science, and mighty achievements in engineering, medicine, and exploration. Many great giants of innovation were laid to rest here, among them William Friese-Green, who was the first to make a moving film on celluloid; Donald Alexander Smith, who helped finance the Canadian Pacific Railway; and Herbert Spencer, who coined the term "survival of the fittest." All around, as you wander, you'll encounter tombs guarded by graceful child angels (for many buried here lived pitifully short lives), yawning lions, and even, rather poetically, a cricketer sleeping under a broken wicket. And then there are the more charming, characterful monuments. One tomb particularly stands out for the oversized statue of a giant mastiff guarding his master's gravesite.

Begin your exploration with the West Cemetery (accessible by guided tour only). Wild, romantic, and in a state of managed neglect, it comprises picturesquely crumbling catacombs and resting places for the wealthy and mighty of Victorian high society. Inside, you'll be shown the gravestone of English poet Christina Rosetti and the burial site of Charles Dickens's clan (Dickens himself is interred at Westminster Abbey). But the pièce de résistance is the approach to the Circle of Lebanon. This begins with Egyptian Avenue, which is dominated by two huge obelisks carved with papyrus and lotus leaves. This gateway leads you through to the Circle, a stone ring of underground structures with doorways surrounding a centuries-old cedar tree. Keep an eye out for the impressive tomb up ahead with its Corinthian columns, modelled on the Mausoleum of Halicarnassus and indicative of the time's self-importance. This is the grave of Julius Beer, financier and owner of the *Observer*. Fittingly, this cemetery, with its lush decay, is also home to many Pre-Raphaelite artists. Its

Opposite: **Waterlow Park**

overgrown tombstones lend an atmosphere that few graveyards can match.

Pass through the ornate iron gates on the opposite side of Swain's Lane to access the East Cemetery. Follow a series of twisting, dark, melancholic footpaths. Stay on the outer path to your left, and be alert for the sight of female English novelist George Eliot's grave. Here you'll also find ❺ KARL MARX'S TOMB, which will be on your right, along the bend; a bust of his bearded head is positioned high above his grave.

Returning to Swain's Lane, take the second gate on the right into Waterlow Park. The park played its part during the First and Second World Wars, providing underground shelters that still exist here. Its three historic ponds are fed by natural springs. Stroll around Middle Pond as you meander the grounds. You'll also come across ❻ LAUDERDALE HOUSE, the 17th-century home of the notorious Earl (later Duke) of Lauderdale. Nell Gwyn, the long-time mistress of Charles II, is said to have been an overnight guest. The building itself dates from the 16th century, as does the garden. Perhaps you'll see the restored wall, part of the terraced garden. Today, the house has its own cafe and al fresco picnic area.

Exit the park by way of Highgate Hill and steer right. Farther down, past Magdala Avenue, pause to admire the scruffy-looking stone cat that casts a wary backward glance at London below. Known as the ❼ WHITTINGTON STONE, this statue marks the site where Dick Whittington "turned once more" toward London. Superstition has it that if the statue is ever removed from this spot, great change and disaster will befall the neighbouring area. Most tales such as this have survived from the days when highwaymen travelled the Great North Road, stopping off at nearby taverns to drink to the stuff of legends.

Continue down the hill until you arrive at Archway Station, on the right. Dare you turn back one last time?

Opposite: Highgate Village

Above: Pond Square, Highgate Village

STARTING POINT
Highgate Underground Station

GETTING THERE
Northern Line, High Barnet branch

1 THE FLASK
77 Highgate West Hill
London N6 6BU
+44 20 8348 7346
www.theflaskhighgate.com

2 SAMUEL TAYLOR
COLERIDGE'S HOME
3 The Grove, London N6 6JU

3 HIGHGATE LITERARY AND
SCIENTIFIC INSTITUTION
11 South Grove, London N6 6BS
+44 20 8340 3343
www.hlsi.net

4 HIGHGATE CEMETERY
Swain's Lane
London N6 6PJ
+44 20 8340 1834
www.highgatecemetery.org

5 KARL MARX'S TOMB
Highgate East Cemetery
Swain's Lane
London N6 6PJ

6 LAUDERDALE HOUSE
Waterlow Park
Highgate Hill
London N6 5HG
+44 20 8348 8716
www.lauderdalehouse.co.uk

7 WHITTINGTON STONE
Highgate Hill (near the intersection
of Magdala Avenue)
London N19 5NE

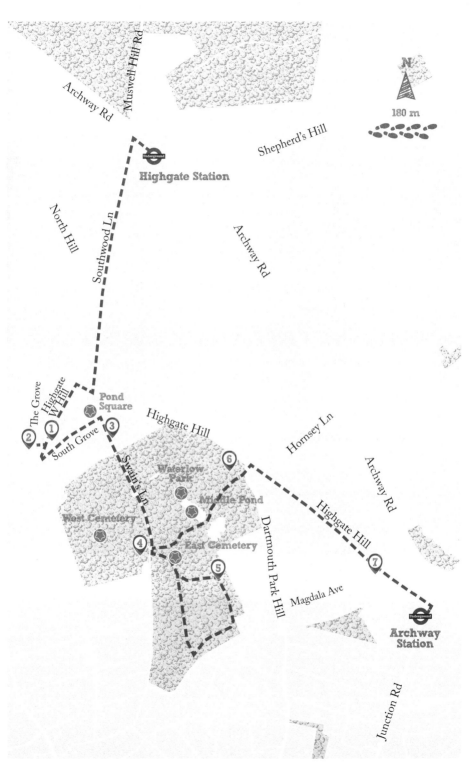

12__ The Utopian Walk

Stoke Newington to Canonbury

BEST TIME: A clear weekend day; wintertime is more atmospheric
DISTANCE: Approximately 4.5 kilometres

Stepping out at Stoke Newington Station onto an inner-city high street with takeaways sandwiched between supermarket chains and saloons, you may feel less than inspired. Keep a lookout, though, for the massive Egyptian-revival-style pillars, which are standing out incongruously, down on your left and across the road. For this is the main entrance to Abney Park, one of the "Magnificent Seven" parkland cemeteries created in the early Victorian period.

Before you venture into the cemetery, a healthy dose of pragmatism will serve you well. Rainy days churn up the muddy soil, so bring the wellies. Not everyone is there to show their respects; some are simply cutting through whilst others may be using the place for unsavoury deals or assignations; best come, therefore, when you're guaranteed fellow strollers. Pick a clear day. Weekends are a good bet. That said, let's depart this mortal coil and cross over into this most alluring and overgrown ancient burial ground.

Following the wide avenue up from the main entrance, you'll pass mighty tombstones and spy angelic statues through the undergrowth. It's spooky, no doubt, but in the best possible way. Whilst there are some more recent graves, with fresh-cut flowers lovingly arranged, the vast majority date back to the mid-19th century. Read the engravings on the stones and you'll spot vaudeville performers alongside top-ranking Salvation Army officers; abolitionists and missionaries; and African royalty and transported slaves. This cemetery was always intended as a resting place for non-conformists, with Stoke Newington having an illustrious history of radical thinking, rabble-rousing, and counterculturalism. The graveyard was also the first to

Opposite: St Mary's Church

Above & Below: **Abney Park cemetery**

be laid out with "no invidious dividing lines" separating the burial areas of one faith or religious group from any other.

You soon arrive at the beautiful ruin of the ❶ OLD ABNEY PARK CHAPEL. One hundred and fifty years ago, this chapel was a feast of Gothic and neoclassical styles. Designed with one central chamber for the common use of all, it became the first nondenominational cemetery chapel in the whole of Europe. All that remains of the building now is a shell. Closed to the public, the ornate plasterwork of the tall windows is crumbling and the roof is patchy. There used to be occult symbols painted on the church, and thirty-odd years ago there were reports of Satanists and witches holding ceremonies here. Today, you're more likely to hear of candlelit tours during Stoke Newington's literary festival than evildoings.

The deeper northwards into the woods you go, the wilder it grows, but also the more haunting and alluring, attracting all kinds of creatures and birds. In certain areas of the park's 32 acres, nature has grown rampantly fecund, with ivy crawling over graves, thick moss enveloping tombs, and weeds half burying paths. I like to imagine this place at the "witching hour," with the Salvation Army band starting up a rousing tune, slaves rising up to dance to their own drum, and music-hall artistes performing for the crowd, while missionaries forget themselves, swaying rhythmically (or not so rhythmically) to the music, and the nameless many emerge from their paupers' graves for a night of free entertainment.

Across from the chapel, you'll spot the dominating statue of the minister and popular hymn writer Isaac Watts. Nearby are tightly packed graves, with barely space for a fist between them. The price for one of these small headstones was around a shilling and for a penny more you could have a name inscribed on it. Being laid to rest here was one step up from a pauper's pit, an unmarked grave where the poor or unclaimed were buried.

Leaving the park for Church Street, you'll pass the perfectly maintained monument to William Booth (1829–1912), social reformer and founder of the Salvation Army. Booth and his wife,

Catherine, are interred here, along with various other high-ranking Christian soldiers.

On Church Street, you'll encounter a grand village vibe, thanks in large part to the absence of a tube connection. Turn right and head in the direction of Clissold Park. The street is lined with independent cafes, junkyards (with bargain antiques), design stores, and the ❹ CHURCH STREET WORKSHOPS, where you can find craftsmen creating and selling their work out of rented studios. Stoke Newington's extensive Turkish community (thanks to a large influx of Turkish immigrants in the 1970s) has spawned a generous number of Ocakbasi restaurants. One of the best is back on Stoke Newington High Street, 19 Numara Bos Cirrik II (No. 194). Along Church Street, I personally rate ❸ LYDIA CAFE for ambience (go here if you have an afternoon to while away with friends) and ❷ CLICIA for breakfast and pleasant service.

Stoke Newington's radicalism is a lot tamer these days, but in its heyday, it was known as "the village that changed the world." Affectionately called Stokey, it has long been a melting pot of innovators, artists, mavericks, and rabble-rousers. It has also attracted some of the greatest writers in history. Daniel Defoe resided on Church Street, where he wrote *Robinson Crusoe* and other famous novels. His presence lives on in the name of Defoe Road, where his blue plaque stands next to a cab office. Between sea voyages, Joseph Conrad returned to his home in nearby Dynevor, and from 1817 to 1820, Edgar Allen Poe was a pupil at the Manor House School, which stood at No. 16 Church Street. These days, the quarter likes to keep the flame alive with the Stoke Newington Literary Festival.

Near the end of Church Street, ❺ STOKE NEWINGTON TOWN HALL is a historic Grade II-listed building with a gorgeous Art Deco façade. It has the folks from the literary festival to thank for its face-lift. Searching for a cheap venue, they alighted on the town hall, which had fallen into near dereliction. The town board told them that they could use the space, provided they restored it.

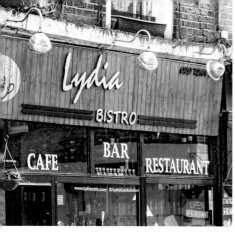

Clockwise from top left: Church Street –
Lydia Bistro, brick building façade, Stoke
Newington Town Hall, Clicia restaurant, row
of shops, Daniel Defoe blue plaque

Above: Shops along Church Street

And that's where the festival spirit kicked in, with some 200 people volunteering their time and labour.

Alongside the town hall, ❻ THE OLD CHURCH, a dainty, ancient-looking house of worship, sits in the shadows of the larger St Mary's across the road. Whilst the building remains consecrated, it also packs in arts events and music concerts. Beyond, Church Street opens outwards to green parkland. Clissold Park looks rather groomed after the higgledy piggledyness of the cemetery, but it too has its redeeming features. It contains two large ornamental lakes, home to many water birds and a population of terrapins, and, quite unexpectedly, a deer enclosure. There are even goats. Below ground, one of London's lost rivers once flowed. During the literary festival, string quartets and circus acts have been known to perform, and families have camped out on midsummer nights.

At the end of the 18th century, Quaker Jonathan Hoare, whose brother Samuel was a leading anti-slave-trade campaigner, built ❼ CLISSOLD HOUSE here. By 1850, Stoke Newington had the

Above: The 18th-century Clissold House in Clissold Park

largest community of Quakers in London. The cafe at Clissold House was recently refurbished and is worth a visit; when the weather is nice, the stately steps outside are perfect for relaxing and watching the world go by.

For your return journey, head through the park to the southwest corner and exit onto Green Lanes. Bear left and walk down to Newington Green, where Mary Wollstencraft – an English writer, original suffragette, and author of *A Vindication of the Rights of Women* – would have crossed over the green to the school for girls she founded with her sister Eliza and friend Fanny Blood in 1784. You can still attend the green's (then radical) ❽ **UNITARIAN CHURCH**, where Wollstencroft would have debated with other outspoken voices of the time, such as Benjamin Franklin, Thomas Paine, and Joseph Priestley.

From here, walk along Ferntower Road, turn left on Petherton Road, and keep going, crossing two roundabouts. You'll find Canonbury BR Station straight on, past the Snooty Fox.

STARTING POINT
Stoke Newington BR Station

GETTING THERE
Overground from Liverpool Street
towards Enfield Town or Cheshunt

1 OLD ABNEY PARK CHAPEL
Abney Park, London N16 0LH

2 CLICIA
97 Stoke Newington Church Street
London N16 0UD
+44 20 7254 1025
www.clician16.com

3 LYDIA CAFE
123 Stoke Newington Church Street
London N16 0UH
+44 20 7249 1386
www.lydiacafe.com

4 CHURCH STREET
WORKSHOPS
Guttridges Yard
172 Stoke Newington Church Street
London N16 0JL
+44 20 7241 3676

5 STOKE NEWINGTON
TOWN HALL
Stoke Newington Church Street
London N16 0JR
+44 20 8356 5505
www.hackneyvenues.com/
stoke-newington-town-hall

6 THE OLD CHURCH
Stoke Newington Church Street
London N16 9ES
www.theoldchurch.org.uk

7 CLISSOLD HOUSE
Stoke Newington Church Street
London N16 9HJ
+44 20 8356 5505
www.hackneyvenues.com/
clissold-house

8 NEW UNITY
Unitarian Church
39A Newington Green
London N16 9PR
+44 20 7354 0774
www.new-unity.org

Left: Abney Park cemetery

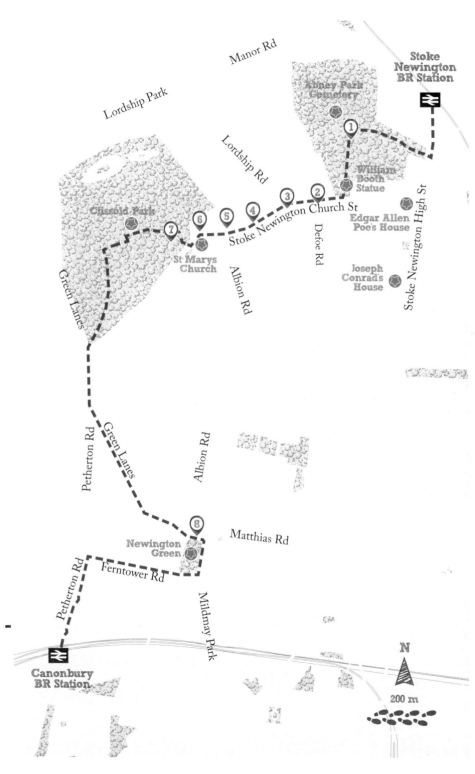

13 The High Society Walk

Hampstead Village

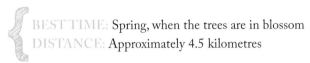

BEST TIME: Spring, when the trees are in blossom
DISTANCE: Approximately 4.5 kilometres

Situated around a large, hilly expanse of parkland and boasting some of the most expensive homes in London, Hampstead Village has long been a draw for the liberal intelligentsia. Counted amongst their number are illustrious artists, musicians, and writers of the 19th and 20th centuries. Step out at Hampstead Heath BR Station, and you are treading in the footsteps of such luminaries as Katherine Mansfield, D H Lawrence, and John Keats, all of whom would have sauntered onto the Heath for exercise or in search of inspiration. Cross-country walkers will enjoy *The Heath Walk* (p. 110), but for those looking to sample society life, let us complete a grand circuit, taking in the full circumference of the village.

Head left out of the station onto South End Road and cross over the pedestrian crossing and turn right, passing the parade of shops (amongst them the highly esteemed travel bookshop ❶ DAUNT BOOKS) before taking the first left down Keats Grove to ❷ NO. 10. The young Romantic poet John Keats came to lodge at this address in 1817 after he met Charles Wentworth Dilke and his friend Charles Brown through poet Leigh Hunt's exclusive circle (Leigh was also to introduce Keats to fellow Romantic poet Percy Bysshe Shelley). Whilst living here, Keats met the love of his life, Fanny Brawne, a member of the Dilke family who resided in adjacent properties. It is said that it was while wandering these gardens that the poet composed "Ode to a Nightingale," amongst other memorable poems. The young lovers became engaged only for Keats to die tragically in Rome of tuberculosis in 1821 before the pair could marry.

Opposite: Plaque on the façade of Keats's House

ERECTED BY THE SOCIETY OF A...

JOHN KEATS,

POET,

LIVED IN THIS HOUSE.

B: 1795.

D: 1821.

Clockwise from top left: The Well Walk Pottery; Hampstead Parish Church burial site; house on Perrin's Court; Keats Grove; façade on Downshire Hill; front door of Keats's House

Leaving Keats Grove for Downshire Hill, make a short detour to the right to ❸ NO. 21, a four-storey end-of-terrace Regency town house where *Vogue* war correspondent Lee Miller lived with surrealist painter Sir Roland Penrose and another lover – in a ménage a trois. Here, they entertained the likes of Picasso when, in the 1930s and early 1940s, the house was known in artistic circles for its parties. A surviving photograph from 1943 of a goose wandering among the guests who were celebrating Miller's birthday touches on the decadence.

Retracing your steps and heading up the hill to Hampstead High Street, you'll find, tucked in between the shops, the single-lane passageway Perrin's Court (just before Waterstones bookstore), which leads through to Fitzjohn's Avenue. This prestigious, tree-lined street has a history of housing noted writers and artists. After 1917, and again in the 1930s, Hampstead became host to a number of émigrés and exiles from the Russian Revolution and Nazi Europe, gaining a reputation for the avant-garde.

Turning onto Church Row, you'll encounter one of the loveliest pockets of Hampstead, with the tower and spire of the Parish Church as backdrop to early 18th-century houses in the Queen Anne style, original wrought-iron gates, and period streetlamps. H G Wells lived at ❹ NO. 17. Here, whilst writing his great comic novel *The History of Mr. Polly*, Wells would have received his great friend George Bernard Shaw as well as the extraordinary talented author Rebecca West, who became Wells's lover.

At ❺ HAMPSTEAD PARISH CHURCH, you'll come upon a picturesque, beautifully kept burial ground; more country churchyard than London cemetery. What makes it all the more enchanting is the fact that the Llewelyn Davies family, whose children inspired J M Barrie's classic, *Peter Pan,* is buried here. Walk downhill from the churchyard along the gravelled Frognal Way and enjoy views over London and a remarkable collection of inter-war villas, including the former home of Gracie Fields, star of both cinema and music hall, at ❻ NO. 20.

Circle back around to the Parish Church, along Church Row, and turn on Holly Walk, which borders the west side of the burial ground. At the end, turn right on Mount Vernon and left on Frognal Rise, then cross the street to Windmill Hill for ❼ BOLTON HOUSE. This was the home of Joanna Baillie (1762–1851), poet and dramatist, one of the first women to be honoured with a blue plaque. Guests who were ushered through these doors would have included the Romantic poets Wordsworth, Byron, and Keats, the last of whom could simply stroll up the hill.

The next street you'll come to is Admiral's Walk, where I urge you to look out for ❽ ADMIRAL'S HOUSE, notable for its roof, which resembles a ship's quarterdeck. The story goes that the admiral who lived here was the inspiration behind the Bankses' neighbour in *Mary Poppins*. The real-life officer, Lieutenant Fountain North, had a ritual of firing a cannon from his rooftop to celebrate royal birthdays and British Naval victories. At street's end, turn right on Hampstead Grove, another glorious-looking Hampstead road with many fine houses and several rewarding byways off of it. ❾ FENTON HOUSE, a National Trust property halfway down the block on your right, is well worth stepping inside for a glimpse of a grand Hampstead period interior and a mosey around the orchard gardens. At the end of the street, you'll be back on Holly Hill.

Dipping down the picturesque back lane of Holly Mount, you'll follow in the footsteps of such illustrious figures as Dickens and Dr Johnson, who would have made their way to the local public house, ❿ THE HOLLY BUSH. Its vintage interior is still lit by gas lamps. After enjoying an ale or something softer, head down Holly Mount Steps for Heath Street.

Cross over to Back Lane, which leads to Flask Walk, where ⓫ THE FLASK pub gleamed a mention in Samuel Richardson's scandalous 18th-century novel *Clarissa*. Tucked alongside the tavern, you'll also spy ⓬ LA CAGE IMAGINAIRE. Hidden away as it is, this little bistro has the protected air of a treasure to which only the locals are privy. Indeed, the whole street has a rather exclusive old-world charm.

Opposite: The historic Flask pub

Above: Flask Walk sign; Below: Keats's House

This next portion of the village, as you amble along Flask Walk, is a personal favourite of mine. Once a fashionable spa town, Hampstead is a reminder of other spa towns, such as Bath and Brighton, with the sheer scale of its grand Regency properties. Up ahead, just before New End Square, is the ⑬ OLD BATHHOUSE, with writing along the frontage that reads, "The Wells &

Campden Trust Bath & Washhouses 1888." At the corner, where Flask Walk turns into Well Walk, you'll arrive at ⑭ BURGH HOUSE. Built in 1703, it once belonged to the daughter of Rudyard Kipling and now houses the Hampstead Museum and a licensed buttery.

To steal a look at the former home of the writer Katherine Mansfield, you'll need to make a loop off of Well Walk via Cannon Lane to Squire's Mount, to ⑮ 17 EAST HEATH ROAD, before continuing on East Heath back around to Well Walk again, for the last portion of your journey.

There is one more novelty to share, at Willow Road, via Christchurch Hill. The house at ⑯ NO. 2, at the bottom of the hill,

Above: The Old Bathhouse on Flask Walk

is another National Trust property, preserving an entirely different period and style – one of which, you sense, Lee Miller and Roger Penrose would have wholly approved. Former family home of the architect Ernö Goldfinger, this modernist house is open to the public and has remained unchanged since 1939. The interior has movable partitions and folding doors and contains a charmingly idiosyncratic collection of art by Max Ernst and Henry Moore. Guided tours are available Wednesday through Sunday.

From here, you can make your way back to Hampstead Heath BR Station via the pretty little stretch of South End Road, which is set off from the main road.

Above: Perrin's Court

STARTING POINT
Hampstead Heath BR Station

GETTING THERE
Overground on Richmond
to Stratford Line

1 DAUNT BOOKS
51 South End Road
London NW3 2QB
+44 20 7794 8206
www.dauntbooks.co.uk

2 JOHN KEATS'S HOUSE
10 Keats Grove, London NW3 2RR
+44 20 7332 3868
www.cityoflondon.gov.uk

3 LEE MILLER'S HOUSE
21 Downshire Hill, London NW3

4 H G WELLS'S HOUSE
17 Church Row, London NW3 6UU

**5 HAMPSTEAD PARISH
CHURCH**
Church Row, London NW3 6UU
+44 20 7794 5808
www.hampsteadparishchurch.org.uk

6 GRACIE FIELDS'S HOUSE
20 Frognal Way, London NW3 6XE

7 BOLTON HOUSE
Windmill Hill, London NW3 6SJ

8 ADMIRAL'S HOUSE
Admiral Walk, London NW3 6RS

9 FENTON HOUSE
Hampstead Grove
London NW3 6SP
+44 20 7435 3471
www.nationaltrust.org.uk

10 THE HOLLY BUSH
22 Holly Mount, London NW3 6SG
+44 20 7435 2892
www.hollybushhampstead.co.uk

11 THE FLASK
14 Flask Walk, London NW3 1HE
+44 20 7435 4580
www.theflaskhampstead.co.uk

12 LA CAGE IMAGINAIRE
16 Flask Walk, London NW3 1HE
+44 20 7794 6674
www.la-cage-imaginaire.co.uk

13 THE OLD BATH HOUSE
75 Flask Walk, London NW3 1ET

**14 BURGH HOUSE &
HAMPSTEAD MUSEUM**
New End Square, London NW3 1LT
+44 20 7431 0144
www.burghhouse.org.uk

**15 KATHERINE MANSFIELD'S
HOUSE**
17 East Heath Road
London NW3 1AL

16 2 WILLOW ROAD
London NW3 1TH
+44 20 7435 6166
www.nationaltrust.org.uk/
2-willow-road

Opposite: A house on Well Walk

Branch Hill

E Heath Rd

Heath St

Squire's Mount

Cannon Ln

15

Lower Terrace

Admiral's Walk

8

Windmill Hill

Hampstead Grove

9

7

New End Sq

14

13

10

Holly Mount Steps

Holly Mount

Back Ln

Flask Walk

Gayton Rd

Holly Walk

12

11

Heath St

Waterstones

Frognal

Church Row

5

Church Row

4

Perrin's Ct

Hampstead High St

Frognal Way

6

Fitzjohn's Ave

Frognal

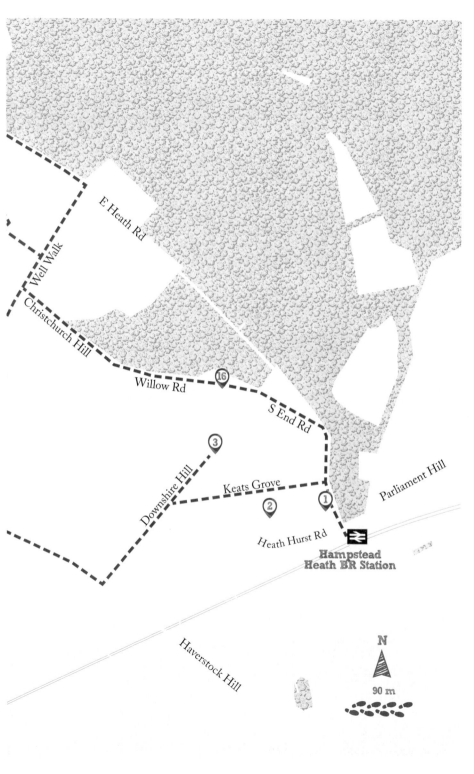

EAST
LONDON

14__ The Street Art Walk

Spitalfields to Shoreditch

BEST TIME: Sunday, for Columbia Road Flower Market
DISTANCE: Approximately 5 kilometres

For centuries, Old Spitalfields has been a haven for the dispossessed. The French Huguenots fled here from religious persecution in the 1700s, whilst the Irish arrived during the potato famine. Later still, it became a refuge for Eastern European Jews who had escaped the Polish pogroms and harsh conditions in Russia. These days, Spitalfields is home to a thriving Bangladeshi community and one of London's liveliest streets: Brick Lane. For a painful period, as recently as the 1980s, the area was abandoned by industry and investment and overrun by the downtrodden and drug addicted. But history teaches us that when a place reaches its saturation point, an implosion occurs, and ushers in change.

First came immigrants selling their treasures and sharing their customs. Then the artists took to the streets, spawning an experimental public art scene, re-envisioning the sides of dilapidated buildings as their canvases. Today, the derelict warehouses have been transformed, hosting an ever-changing procession of modern and vintage fashion, saris, and street food fairs and markets, orbiting around the largest of them all, Old Spitalfields Market, which packs in more than a hundred stalls under a huge trussed and glazed roof canopy.

To access this fine Victorian hall, simply exit Liverpool Street Station on busy Bishopsgate, head north, and turn right on Brushfield Street. Far back into the 17th and 18th centuries, the encompassing area was the heartland of the country's silk industry, and the sprawling market is located just across the road from the old weavers' houses on Brushfield. Before entering the the market, experience a historical re-imagining of a home belonging to a family of Huguenot silk weavers:

Opposite: **Graffiti art on Whitby Street**

Clockwise from top left: Old Weavers' Warehouses on Fournier Street; Sunday Upmarket; Old Spitalfields Market; Vintage Market sign; Brick Lane street art

turn up Bishops Square, which is the path between the Goat Statue and Patisserie Valerie, cross over to Spital Square, and turn left on Folgate Street. ❶ DENNIS SEVERS' HOUSE is tucked in back of the market hall. To enter the main market, simply head back to where Bishops and Spital Squares meet, turn left, and then take the first right, on Crispin Place.

❷ OLD SPITALFIELDS MARKET specializes in different areas depending on the day of the week. On Thursdays, it becomes an antiques fair featuring dealers from all over the country. Fridays are fashion focused. Saturdays vary in theme but you're guaranteed a mix of vintage and designer products. On Sundays, the market showcases the work of college design graduates. Mondays, Tuesdays, and Wednesdays are less crowded, with a combination of apparel, footwear, gifts, and bric-a-brac.

Leaving the coverage of Crispin Place for Fournier Street, slip past the Gothic steeple and Tuscan columns of ❸ CHRIST CHURCH SPITALFIELDS, designed by Nicholas Hawksmoor, a leading figure of the English Baroque architectural style from the late 17th to early 18th century. Across the street from the church is ❹ THE TEN BELLS pub, forever linked to the Jack the Ripper story, as two of his victims, Annie Chapman and Mary Jane Kelly, were regular customers. The notorious Whitechapel district, where the infamous serial killer roamed, starts just down the street. Most of his crime scenes have been redeveloped several times over now, removing any traces of the cobbled streets and horse-drawn carriages of Victorian London.

As you make your way along Fournier Street, gaze upon the old ❺ WEAVERS' WAREHOUSES with their colourful bricks, mansard garrets, and weather-boarded fronts. Built to accommodate the master silk weavers, these well-appointed terraced buildings were once a hive of activity, filled with workers weaving, cutting, and dying silk. The uppermost floors were occupied by the weavers because they offered the best light for the looms, while the ground floors served as elaborate showrooms for the finished products.

You'll know you've arrived at Brick Lane by the Indian restaurateurs jostling with each other for your custom on the pavement. High up on every corner are the street names in both English and Bengali, as well as some cheeky subversive graffiti tags. Turn left onto the lane, and you'll encounter a rather plain-looking Georgian building dating back to 1743, with a curious anomaly: a huge rocket-shaped minaret outside. ❻ BRICK LANE JAMME MASJID MOSQUE serves the largest concentration of Bangladeshi Muslims in the country. Over its 275-year history, this house of worship has morphed from a Huguenot chapel to a church for Methodists and Protestants to a synagogue and now a mosque. There is something beautiful about how this spot has been absorbing immigrants and refugees of all nationalities and religions for centuries. Cross the street to best observe the sundial, set high up on the mosque's wall, and read its Latin inscription, *Umbra sumus*, which hauntingly translates as, "We are shadow."

Around the corner, behind the shabby front doors of one of London's smallest historic buildings, ❼ 19 PRINCELET STREET is a unique cultural organization: a crucible for the area's multi-faceted immigration stories – a museum of immigration, if you will. It is a rare privilege to go inside, and if you are fortunate enough to be there on an occasion when it opens its doors to the public (in June for Refugee Week, for example), you will discover one remarkable story after another, as the fragile objects of generation after generation of immigrants stack up, beginning with the Jews. At the end of Princelet, turn right on Wilkes Street. Up ahead, the crowds flow east along Hanbury Street towards another popular indoor market on Brick Lane, known as ⓫ SUNDAY UPMARKET. Before joining them, look west on Hanbury and you'll spot the giant representation of a stork painted leeside of a derelict building. All around, street art is in plain view, down side alleys, beneath the windows on storefronts, directly across from you in doorways, or high above on parapets. Take time to observe the fleeting images painted by anonymous artists working in the shadows: the wizened old face of

Above: Brick Lane; Below: Hanbury Street wall art

Above & Below: Shops along Brick Lane

an elder, red roses that morph into a Lenin-esque portrait, elephants performing a circus act over a ledge. There is so much to absorb, for the richness of this place reveals itself slowly. Self-expression is too tiny a word for what has happened here; necessity is the mother of invention, the old saying goes.

In keeping with the street's edgy vibe, you'll also find yourself in retro fashion heaven here. There's ❽ ABSOLUTE VINTAGE at No. 15 (across from the delectable Rosa's Thai Cafe Spitalfields) and ❾ BLITZ LONDON at No. 55 – 59. And back on Brick Lane, at No. 85, ascend the staircase and you'll discover a veritable Aladdin's cave at the ❿ VINTAGE MARKET, with specialists from all over Europe ready to enthral with garments packed into a huge warehouse space, open Friday through Sunday. You'll come across even more vintage clothing down Cheshire Street, off Brick Lane, with stores like ⓬ LEVISONS at No. 1 and ⓭ BEYOND RETRO at No. 110 –112.

Here, fashion only comes in second to one thing: food – or maybe we'll call it a draw. As you steer north among the famed curry houses lining Brick Lane, it is not long before the street food markets take over, with one vendor selling paella, another falafel or Caribbean fare. One place not to be missed is the Jewish-style ⓮ BEIGEL BAKE. As it is open 24 hours, a late-night visit to this spot has become something of a native Londoner's rite of passage – with clubbers and cab drivers making a special detour here in the early hours of Saturday and Sunday mornings. After the decline of London's silk weaving industry, this whole neighbourhood became the heart of the Jewish East End. On Friday nights – the eve of the Sabbath – candles would be seen burning in parlour windows. In the early 20th century, when the Spitalfields Jewish community was at its peak, there were more than 15 kosher butchers, as well as shops selling bagels, salted herring, and other Jewish delicacies.

Leaving the chaotic vibrancy of Brick Lane behind, cross over into Shoreditch by way of Redchurch Street and continue to keep an eye out for some lingering artistic daubs on the sides of buildings. Turn

Above: London's famous Brick Lane

right on Club Row towards Arnold Circus. The renovated redbrick tenements that fan out from this central roundabout comprise a listed Arts and Crafts estate. Arnold Circus is where residents can come to get away from the throng, making their way to ⑮ ROCHELLE CANTEEN, a cafe and restaurant hidden behind the wall of the neighbourhood school in the former bike shed.

In keeping with the area's vibrant past, our last stop is the weekly ⑯ COLUMBIA ROAD FLOWER MARKET. Come off the Circus at Hocker Street, make a right on Virginia Road, and follow the bend of the street around to Columbia Road. Turn right and walk along for 200 metres, until the scent of fresh-cut flowers overpowers you. The market was moved to Sunday in order to accommodate the needs of local Jewish traders. This, in turn, allowed Spitalfields vendors to sell their leftover stock from Saturday. Interestingly, it was the Huguenot immigrants who introduced an interest in cut flowers and plants, together with a fascination for caged songbirds (the pub at the end of the market is fittingly called the Birdcage). It's the merchandise and the bohemian, artsy vibe that keep bringing people back to Columbia Road. All year round, you get to enjoy this Victorian street in full bloom, a confection of colours.

To make your way home, head for Brawn cafe on the corner of Columbia Road and Ravenscroft Street, and walk up Ravenscroft. At the top, make a left on Hackney Road and take the second right, on Cremer Street, then another right on Geffrye Street, for Hoxton BR Station.

Opposite: Columbia Road Flower Market

STARTING POINT
Liverpool Street Underground Station

GETTING THERE
Central, Circle,
or Hammersmith & City Lines

1 DENNIS SEVERS' HOUSE
18 Folgate Street, London E1 6BX
+44 20 7247 4013
www.dennissevershouse.co.uk

2 OLD SPITALFIELDS MARKET
16 Horner Square, London E1 6EW
+44 20 7426 0246
www.oldspitalfieldsmarket.com

3 CHRIST CHURCH
SPITALFIELDS
Commercial Street, London E1 6LY
+44 20 7377 2440
www.ccspitalfields.org

4 THE TEN BELLS
84 Commercial Street
London E1 6LY
+44 20 7247 7532
www.tenbells.com

5 WEAVERS' WAREHOUSES
Fournier Street, London E1 6QE

6 BRICK LANE MOSQUE
59 Brick Lane, London E1 6QL
+44 20 7247 6052
www.bricklanejammemasjid.co.uk

7 19 PRINCELET STREET
London E1 6QH
+44 20 7247 5352
www.19princeletstreet.org.uk

8 ABSOLUTE VINTAGE
15 Hanbury Street, London E1 6QR
+44 20 7247 3883
www.absolutevintage.co.uk

9 BLITZ LONDON
55–59 Hanbury Street
London E1 5JP
+44 20 7377 0730
www.blitzlondon.co.uk

10 VINTAGE MARKET
The Old Truman Brewery
85 Brick Lane, London E1 6QL
+44 20 7770 6028
www.vintage-market.co.uk

11 SUNDAY UPMARKET
The Old Truman Brewery
91 Brick Lane
London E1 6QL
+44 20 7770 6000
www.sundayupmarket.co.uk

12 LEVISONS
1 Cheshire Street
London E2 6ED
+44 20 3609 2224
www.levisons.co.uk

13 BEYOND RETRO
110–112 Cheshire Street
London E2 6EJ
+44 20 7729 9001
www.beyondretro.com

14 BEIGEL BAKE
159 Brick Lane
London E1 6SB
+44 20 7729 0616

15 ROCHELLE CANTEEN
Rochelle School, Arnold Circus
London E2 7ES
+44 20 7729 5667
www.arnoldandhenderson.com

16 COLUMBIA ROAD FLOWER
MARKET
Columbia Road
London E2 7RG
www.columbiaroad.info

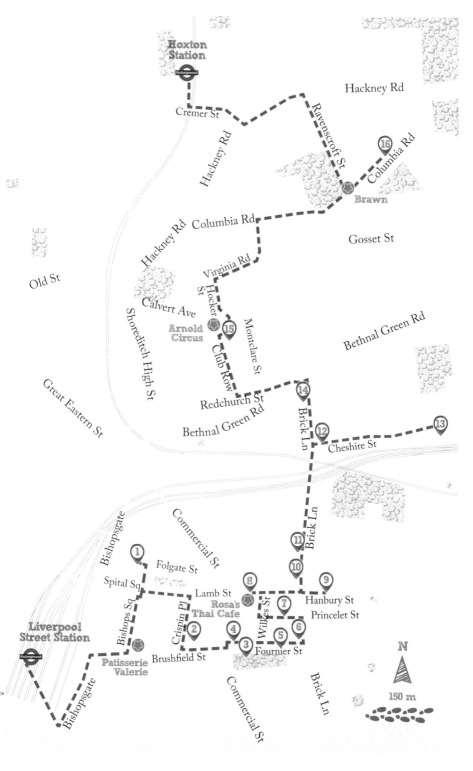

15__ The Restoration Walk

Shoreditch to Barbican

BEST TIME: Sunday afternoon, for Barbican rooftop conservatory; Thursday or Friday, for Whitecross Street Special Food Market
DISTANCE: Approximately 3 kilometres

Much like New York City's meatpacking district, Shoreditch has undergone major regeneration and urban renewal since the millennium. Before the creative and media trades moved in (converting former industrial buildings into open-plan offices and designer hotels), this tiny grid of streets was crammed with furniture makers and woodcutters. A predominantly working-class area, it attracted young designers and artists, like Tracey Emin, who seized on the neighbourhood's cheap rents and warehouse spaces. That's when the hype ratcheted up, and the cool kids wanted in. First came Shoreditch House, a boutique hotel, followed closely by Sir Terence Conran's restaurant, Boundary. Ever spinning, the East End oscillates between those creating a designer aesthetic – a lifestyle, and those who would uphold tradition, and their livelihoods.

From the Shoreditch tube station, take a left on Bethnal Green, followed by a quick right on Ebor Street, to Redchurch Street. Here you'll find beaten-looking minicab firms alongside flagship stores and boutique hotels, while hipsters compete with local teenagers for pavement space. At No. 85, the old Dolphin Pub is now ❶ **LABOUR AND WAIT**, the vision of owners Simon Watkins and Rachel Wythe-Moran, who say they had grown tired of over-designed gimmicky products and decided to relocate their hardware store here, blending their commitment to selling quality long-lasting items with the design aesthetic of their adopted neighbourhood.

Stroll along Turville and Montclare Streets and note the attractive redbrick tenements all around, which are part of a listed Arts and Crafts

Opposite: Labour and Wait

Clockwise from top left: Syd's coffee stall; listed Arts & Craft estate; street art; Barber & Parlour salon; Shoreditch Old Town Hall

estate, originally built as social housing when the slums around here were cleared out in the early 1900s. The Boundary Estate's centrepiece is the impressive old bandstand at Arnold Circus, which was returned to its former glory by the Friends of Arnold Circus, a community group. For decades, this neighbourhood had a reputation for vandalism and street crime, and so, in the 1990s, the area was cleared again; only this time, social housing was replaced by private ownership.

Coming off the Circus onto the rather sleek, chic Calvert Avenue, appearing more like a street one might find in Chelsea rather than EC1, look out for Leila's, a trendy grocery-store-cum-coffeehouse at No.15–17, a few doors away from Ally Capellino at No. 9, a shop known for luxurious leather goods. But it is the horse-drawn carriage parked down the road that is the prize. This is ❷ SYD'S coffee stall, an East End landmark, which has been serving locals and cab drivers since 1919. These days, it is run by Jane Tothill, granddaughter of the original owner – a World War I veteran who used his pension to open the small stand all those years ago.

As you move into the hub of Shoreditch, just up ahead is Shoreditch High Street. This short stretch to the north includes a vibrant mix of hip cafes and high-end shops catering to City workers' bank accounts. Past the railway bridge, Kingsland Road becomes something of a wasteland (with the notable exception of a few terrific Vietnamese restaurants and the Geffrye Museum), so turn instead onto Old Street, whose centrepiece is ❸ SHOREDITCH TOWN HALL. Closed way back in the 1960s, the building was saved from developers and reopened as a giant arts centre. Exciting independent theatre companies like dreamthinkspeak are re-imagining how spaces like this can be used for interactive productions, staging performances that draw audiences into the deepest recesses of the 150-year-old edifice. The motto "More Light, More Power" is inscribed on the walls. Rather fittingly for your walk, the statue on the tower outside is dedicated to "Progress."

Continuing to the fork in the road, bear right toward Hoxton Square. Once located at No. 48, ❹ WHITE CUBE gallery, which exhibited the likes of avant-garde English artists Gilbert and George, has relocated south of the river, but the original building still stands. The 1920s light industrial building was transformed into a white two-tier space by Jay Jopling in 2002. Further along on Coronet Street, city workers can swap their desks at lunchtime for a trapeze at the ❺ NATIONAL CENTRE FOR CIRCUS ARTS. Housed in the former Shoreditch Electric Light Station, which opened in 1896, the interior retains features of its former life including the magnificent combustion and generating chambers.

A left on Pitfield and a right on Old Street will lead to the Old Street traffic circle (known locally as Silicon Roundabout because of the number of technology companies moving into the neighbourhood). Don't be fooled by the quaint name, though – even the *thought* of walking around here wears me down, with the area's concentrated volume of traffic and multiple exit routes flying off in all directions; but take this as a quick means to an end. Make your way west, off the third exit, to remain on Old Street, and you can look forward to experiencing the city within a city at the Barbican; a brutalist masterpiece to some and an eyesore to others, but unanimously a world-class arts centre.

Along the way, you'll pass ❻ ST LUKE'S, a deconsecrated church which is home to the London Symphony Orchestra. The original church was built in 1733 and its distinguishing feature – an obelisk spire – was the work of the Baroque-inspired English architect Nicolas Hawksmoor. In back, you'll find St Luke's Garden, which overlooks the Ironmonger Row Baths, a former public bath that was renovated and reopened as a community leisure facility. Staying true to tradition, the work included the restoration of the old Turkish bath area.

Across the road from the church is Whitecross Street – the kind of place that is known locally but doesn't get much attention outside the neighbourhood. The street, which dates back to medieval times, is

Opposite: National Centre for Circus Arts

Above & Below: The Barbican Centre

now best known for its food market, and for its yearly festival of urban art. The name harks back to a white cross that was erected around 1000 AD after the area was developed. Located just beyond the walls of London, the street wasn't beholden to the city's rules governing trade and as such was unregulated. The ❼ WHITECROSS STREET SPECIAL FOOD MARKET, where you can sample a wide variety of cuisines from around the world, is open every Thursday and Friday, from 11am to 5pm. Check the online calendar for the Whitecross Street Party, usually held in the summer, accompanied by a six-week street art exhibition. It is one of London's most unique public events, and a great family-friendly outing. For a taste of the urban art scene all year round, check out ❽ CURIOUS DUKE GALLERY, which plays host to exhibitions of some of the best up and coming artists, on the corner of Banner Street.

At street's end, you'll spot the Jugged Hare public house. Slip down Silk Street and you'll be on the threshold of the ❾ BARBICAN CENTRE, set within beautiful gardens amidst sections of the old Roman city hall. For residents (there are 4000 people living here in more than 2000 apartments), the Barbican offers the amenities of a town centre, including a school and a launderette. Local volunteers even run a heritage salvage store, where they accumulate the estate's original fittings, so those who still have the old kitchens and bathrooms can try and match them up. As with Marmite, you'll either love the architecture or loathe it.

Enter the Barbican on Silk Street and head up to the podium level to reach Gilbert Bridge, which looks down on the lake and terrace below. The bridge runs between the massive columns that hold up the apartment block Gilbert House. Viewed quixotically, the centre has something of a medieval street layout: elevated walkways interconnect the complex, towers loom, and the architecture has an incredible curvature. Surprises abound, such as the sight of the Grade I-listed church of ❿ ST GILES across the ornamental lake. This is where Oliver Cromwell was married and the poet John Milton was interred. Then there are the places you wouldn't stumble across unless you were in the know. Back inside the main centre, head up to the roof on level 4. Here you'll discover a magnificent conservatory, to rival Kew, below a glass roof, housing an unbelievable assortment of tropical plants, birds, and a fish pond. Admission to the conservatory is free but public opening times are very limited: currently only on Sunday afternoons and some bank holiday Mondays. When you want to leave the centre, return to Silk Street and take a left down into the tunnel, resurfacing across the street from the Barbican's tube stop.

STARTING POINT
Shoreditch High Street BR Station

GETTING THERE
Overground from Highbury & Islington

① LABOUR AND WAIT
85 Redchurch Street
London E2 7DJ
+44 20 7729 6253
www.labourandwait.co.uk

② SYD'S
Calvert Avenue
London E1 6JN

③ SHOREDITCH TOWN HALL
380 Old Street
London EC1V 9LT
+44 20 7739 6176
www.shoreditchtownhall.com

④ FORMER WHITE CUBE GALLERY
48 Hoxton Street
London N1
+44 20 7930 5373
www.whitecube.com

⑤ NATIONAL CENTRE FOR CIRCUS ARTS
Coronet Street, London N1 6HD
+44 20 7613 4141
www.nationalcircus.org.uk

⑥ LSO ST LUKE'S
161 Old Street, London EC1V 9NG
+44 20 7490 3939
www.lso.co.uk

⑦ WHITECROSS STREET MARKET
13 Whitecross Street
London EC1Y 8JL

⑧ CURIOUS DUKE GALLERY
173 Whitecross Street
London EC1Y 8JT
+44 20 7251 6551
www.curiousdukegallery.com

⑨ BARBICAN CENTRE
Silk Street, London EC2Y 8DS
+44 20 7638 4141
www.barbican.org.uk

⑩ ST GILES CRIPPLEGATE
Fore Street, London EC2Y 8DA
+44 20 7638 1997
www.stgilescripplegate.com

Opposite: The Barbican Centre

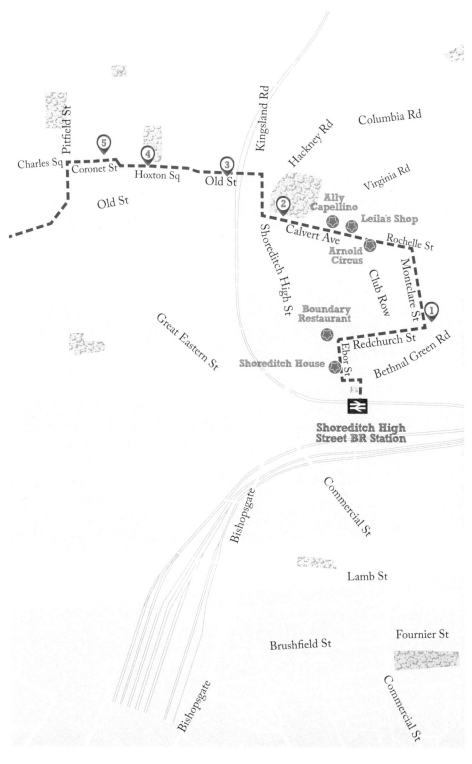

 The Canal Walk

Islington to Victoria Park

BEST TIME: Spring or summer
DISTANCE: Approximately 6.5 kilometres

Nowhere can you peer behind London's façade better than on a canal walk. Only here, amidst the snowdrops and grime, the narrow boats and tow bridges, do you get a sense of where the metropolis's gypsy-hearted roost. Arrive on the Victorian-built Upper Street at Angel, Islington, and observe the unusually high one-metre pavements. These were constructed in the 1860s to protect pedestrians from being splashed by the large number of cattle passing along the coach route to the north. But long before that, these were fields for pasture and open meadows into which the river waters flowed, mills turned and, beyond, an immense forest grew. In the 1700s, this area was known far and wide as London's dairy. Among the more prosperous farmers was Samuel Rhodes, great-grandfather of the Rhodesian statesman Cecil Rhodes. Tea gardens blossomed around rediscovered springs, and the air at Islington was considered so good that it was known as London's hospital. Incredibly, even after the 19th century, when builders and speculators turned the hay fields into a quagmire of roads and tenement buildings, one can still rediscover a place that refreshes dulled spirits; you only have to get off the beaten track.

For that, you'll need to come off at Duncan Street near Camden Passage. When you reach the vine-covered iron railings at the end of the street, peer over the bridge and you'll see the eastern stretch of the Regent's Canal. Head down the steps to your left. At first glance, London, with her skyscrapers, tower blocks, and flyovers, may not seem the most accommodating of places for an Arcadian walk, but never underestimate the locals' spirit to work with what they have. Throughout the capital, there are still swathes of fertile ground. As

Opposite: Regent's Canal

All pictures: Sights and scenes along Regent's Canal and the towpath.

you progress, Georgian terraces are replaced by council housing, for much of this area was damaged during the Blitz.

I won't pretend it's an idyllic beginning, what with 21st-century waterside property developments competing alongside council estates, but catch sight of a local inhabitant clambering aboard a snug narrow boat moored along the canal, or a deck festooned with pots and well-watered plants, and suddenly life here doesn't seem so grim. Watch out for millennial East Londoners; they'll be popping up like poppies along this route. You can identify them by their fine blend of utilitarian clothing with a dandifying touch.

All year round, multi-hued barges are moored along the canal but, on a summer's day, their owners truly revel in their adopted gypsy lifestyle, hosting small, lively onboard gatherings or jauntily motoring along. In springtime, the grassy knolls are sprinkled with snowdrops and the magnolia trees are in full bloom. Charm can be found in even the grimiest of settings (though, charming or not, it's inadvisable to be wandering down by the canal after dark). A mile and half into the walk, approximately 30 minutes, the towpath begins to liven up. First comes the ❶ TOWPATH CAFE, a popular local haunt that's open seasonally from March to November. The seating is a covered alcove, open to the elements, which makes it the perfect place to shelter on wet days or get out of the sun and into the shade on warmer ones. Several doors down is ❷ PROUD EAST, a gallery, cinema room, and restaurant. Around the corner, opposite the Waterhouse – a restaurant and terrace that gives local young people the chance to work in the food industry – is ❸ KINGSLAND BASIN. At first it looks like any other stark canal-side development, but investigate further, and you'll discover that a community of boaters have spawned their own vegetable allotment here, in a specially adapted garden barge.

A couple of bridges on, you'll pass under Broadway Market, which is well worth a gander (check out the *East End Market Lovers' Walk*, p. 216), but this walk concentrates on escaping commercial London, and so, onwards my friends, to the People's Park, more widely known as Victoria Park. From here, I can say, with hand on heart, the environs improve considerably. Trees prosper. Well-kept back gardens slope down to the water. Even the narrow boats appear more spruced up. It all becomes rather bucolic.

Follow the path into the park, keeping parallel to the river, and you'll be greeted by the fearsome statues of the *Dogs of Alcibiades*. Wander down the wide tree-lined avenue, and laze in one of the discrete enclosures at your leisure, before crossing over the small arched bridge towards the ➍ CHINESE PAGODA, which emerges from the trees across the ornamental West Boating Lake and is a lovely spot in which to meditate or relax and enjoy the ambient surroundings. Make your way around the lake to the ➎ PAVILION, a domed-shaped cafe which offers beautiful panoramic views across the lake and the park.

Only then, as you survey the grounds, might you dare to picture the lawns trampled underfoot by captured German and Italian soldiers, when the park was repurposed as an internment camp during World War II. You may also try to imagine the scene in 1912, when the suffragette Sylvia Pankhurst was drawing in the crowds at Speaker's Corner; or more than 170 years ago, when this park wasn't even an idea in architect Sir James Pennethorne's head. Back then, all this was an East End slum, where disease was rife and the poverty stricken were left to wallow in their own filth.

But it is not all doom and gloom, for the park arose out of a noble ambition to provide fresh air and open green spaces for the East End's poor. For many, this would have been the only patch of nature they saw their entire lives. Other honourable pursuits followed, including socialist political meetings and rallies throughout the 19th and 20th centuries.

North-east of the park is Lauriston Road, which leads into the heart of gentrified Victoria Park Village. Whilst others stroll to the nearby delis and cake shops, let us remain with the past a moment longer and head south-east instead, exiting the park on Old Ford Road and crossing over the canal. Nearing the end of Old Ford Road, be on the lookout for ➏ THE GALLERY CAFE, situated in a Georgian

Opposite: Chinese Pagoda, Victoria Park

town house of real character and charm. You can tell by looking at the building that it has a story. It was formerly a ladies' mission, where suffragettes did pioneering work that included initiatives towards workers' welfare, employment for very poor women, nursing the sick, assistance for mothers, and running clubs for girls. To this day, the mission supports community groups. Inside, the attractively bohemian cafe is a cosy place to squirrel away in winter, and come summer, its garden doors are flung open so customers and regulars can enjoy the terrace suntrap in back.

At street's end, turn left onto busy Cambridge Heath Road. The built-up inner-city surroundings may feel rather jarring after our canal-side idyll, but I've pulled you off course for good reason. See that magnificent Grade II-listed Victorian building ahead? That is the ❼ V&A MUSEUM OF CHILDHOOD. Home to one of the world's finest collections of children's toys, dollhouses, games, and costumes, it is a remarkable space which boasts many original 19th-century features, including the elegant and historic Marble Floor. The story goes that female inmates of Woking Gaol laid the fish-scale-patterned floor, piece by piece. Once you've done a turn around the museum, bear left out of the exit and keep walking until you reach the steps heading down to Bethnal Green Underground Station.

STARTING POINT
Angel Underground Station
GETTING THERE
Northern Line

❶ TOWPATH CAFE
36 De Beauvoir Crescent, London N1 5SB
+44 20 7254 7606

❷ PROUD EAST
2–10 Hertford Road, London N1 5ET
+44 20 7647 6712
www.proudeast.com

❸ KINGSLAND BASIN
London N1

❹ CHINESE PAGODA
Victoria Park, London E3 5TB

❺ PAVILION
Crown Gate West, Victoria Park
London E9 7DE
+44 20 8980 0030

❻ THE GALLERY CAFE
St. Margaret's House
21 Old Ford Road
London E2 9PL
+44 20 8980 2092
www.stmargaretshouse.org.uk

❼ V&A MUSEUM
OF CHILDHOOD
Cambridge Heath Road
London E2 9PA
+44 20 8983 5200
www.vam.ac.uk

Above: Canal boat; Below: Victoria Park

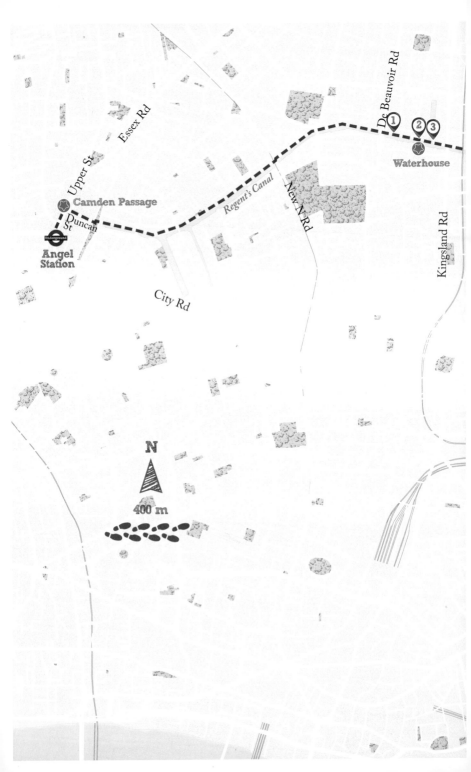

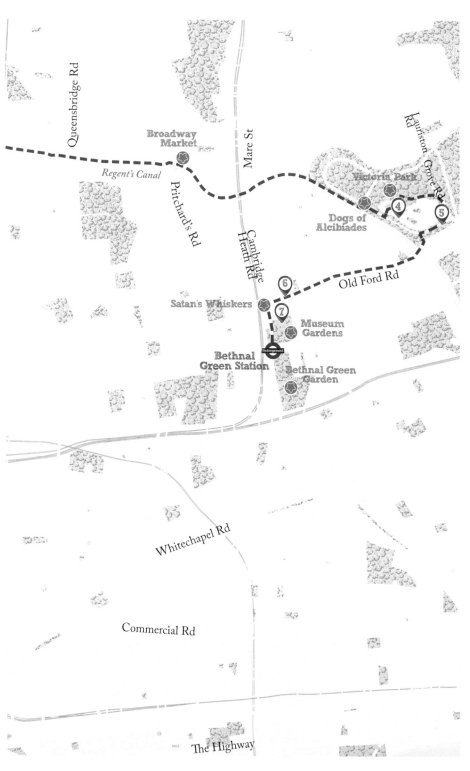

17__ The Wharves Walk

St Katharine's Dock to Wapping to Canary Wharf

 BEST TIME: A clear day, for the best views
DISTANCE: Approximately 6 kilometres

As you descend the steps at Tower Hill, the Tower of London may well dominate the view ahead, but queens and kings play no part in this outing. No, where you are heading is into the realm of naval officers and mariners, dockers, and manufacturers. For at one time, the banks of the River Thames played home to more than 1,700 wharves, a testament to the industry necessary to build an empire.

Circumnavigating the castle, move east, and you'll catch sight of a vivid splash of colour: the royal blue of Tower Bridge. As you cross over Tower Bridge Approach to St Katharine's Way, take in the view of the Shard, the tallest building in London, rising in the distance. For this is a stroll that observes the markers of London's grand trading past – and its spoils.

A few yards along St Katharine's Way, be on the lookout for a discreet staircase down to St Katharine Docks. The last thing you'd expect to find is a working marina, hidden from view, and the most tranquil of havens nestled in the centre of the city, but here you are. Gleaming white super-yachts are moored imperiously against the backdrop of renovated old wharf buildings. Hidden beneath these six-storeyed warehouses, which surround you on all sides, extensive vaults once held thousands of casks of valuable wine and other luxury goods that poured into the docks on a daily basis.

Passing popular restaurants Strada and Tom's Kitchen, you'll reach the Medieval Banqueting Hall. Step along the causeway and through the archway to enter the heart of the marina. Turn left and across the lock you'll spy an attractive timber-framed building, ❶ THE DICKENS INN. From its porch and balconies, you have the best

Opposite: The Dickens Inn

of vantage points. Back in Elizabethan times, these docks would have been all hustle and bustle as seafaring men sallied forth to this nearby tavern whilst the dockworkers unloaded such precious cargo as barrels of rum from the West Indies, ivory from Africa, marble from Europe and, of course, tea from the Far East.

Follow the path around to Mews Street and rejoin St Katharine's Way, which turns into Wapping High Street, where you'll spy a remnant of the medieval Hermitage Wall. Whilst you could take a shortcut along the ornamental canal in back to Tobacco Docks, you'd be trading the richness of the old wharves and vestiges of the merchant capital of the 1700s for a rather soulless new-build estate. Instead, elect to walk the length of Wapping High Street. Gradually the new buildings fall away, replaced by elegant, sooty-looking Georgian terrace houses, your first sighting of which will be near ❷ PIER HEAD, with its railings cutting off the row of homes set around a queer-looking, barren square. In fact this was once the main maritime entrance of the London Docks, where customs officers and wealthy merchants would keep a watchful eye on the ships entering and leaving. You'll see many more such examples as you advance through Wapping.

You won't want to miss ❸ WAPPING OLD STAIRS, by the side of Town of Ramsgate public house. This narrow passage leads down to the Thames foreshore, but only at low tide, and only via some very dilapidated steps. Here you can still observe the post where condemned pirates were chained to drown as the tide rose.

Turn off at Wapping Lane for ❹ TOBACCO DOCK, a store for imported tobacco some 200 years ago. You'll know you've arrived when you spot the two replica ships by the canal. The first, the *Three Sisters*, would have sailed back from the East and West Indies with tobacco and spices. The second, the *Sea Lark*, is modelled on the American merchant schooner captured by the Royal Navy during the Anglo-American War. Check out the

Opposite: New Crane Wharf

seven-foot-tall bronze sculpture of a child standing in front of a tiger. The statue pays tribute to an incident in the late 1800s, when a wild Bengal tiger escaped from the world's largest exotic pet shop, located nearby, and carried off a small boy who had approached and tried to touch the animal. The boy escaped unhurt after the store owner gave chase and prised open the animal's jaws with his bare hands.

Now head east along the canal, passing through Wapping Woods, until you reach ❺ SHADWELL BASIN. Savour the incredible view across the water to Canary Wharf, the shimmering towers of Citibank and HSBC standing head, shoulders, and knees above their neighbours.

Keep to the path right of the basin, and turn right at Wapping Wall, where the businesses in the area were once boat builders and navigation equipment manufacturers, and all the other trades necessary for maritime activity. On your left will be ❻ THE PROSPECT OF WHITBY public house, where the great English writers Charles Dickens and Samuel Pepys were known to drink (that Dickens did get around). The interior is attractively laid out like the captain's quarters of a 17th-century full-rigged ship. Once known as Devil's Tavern, this was a meeting place for sailors, smugglers, and cut-throats.

But the real find here is across the street. If you weren't on the lookout for it, you could well walk right by the industrial-looking ❼ WAPPING HYDRAULIC POWER STATION, which received a new lease on life when it was transformed into an art space with images projected onto the building's exposed brick walls. What is so refreshing, however, is the consideration afforded the viewing public. Outside, the organisers have set up an area for serving free cups of tea and coffee, whilst inside, they've devoted an entire antechamber to a "chill-out room," where a long library-style table is covered in art and photography books. Pull up a chair and pore over images by Annie Leibovitz and Henri Cartier-Bresson at your leisure. The greatest surprise awaits you around the side entrance,

Clockwise from top left: City skyscrapers; wharves; Prospect of Whitby public house; West India Quay; view across the river of Canary Wharf; Tower Bridge

where you'll find the old engine house with much of the original equipment perfectly preserved – a true rarity.

Next up, make your way back past Shadwell Basin and along Wapping Wall and take the second right, following signs for the Thames Path. Along the path, look for another glimpse of the Shard to the west, whose dimensions shape-shift, and Canary Wharf to the east. After about 500 metres, the path merges into Narrow Street, which continues to run parallel to the river.

How I admire this stretch in the back of Limehouse, where the picturesque buildings and river setting have proven a magnet for artists and writers. Interestingly, back in the 1960s, writer Andrew Sinclair bought and saved one of these early Georgian houses upon finding the area derelict and abandoned. Sinclair then persuaded his Cambridge friends to purchase the others. Naughtily, I can't resist peeping through the windows of several of the gorgeously painted homes that run alongside the well-regarded public house ❾ THE GRAPES and ❽ THE NARROW gastropub, one of celebrity chef Gordon Ramsey's fleet of London restaurants. The Grapes (again frequented by a young Dickens) was, notably, bought in 2011 by the actor Sir Ian McKellan.

Rejoining the Thames Path by way of Three Colt Street, about 300 metres on from the Grapes, you are mere moments away from Canary Wharf. Here is the true pinnacle of what the maritime trade achieved. This silver city. This Oz. Incredible to believe that these Manhattan-style quays were the departure point for the *Mayflower*, which brought the English to the colonies in 1620.

Cross straight over the roundabout at Westferry Circus to West India Avenue and you're moving into the epicentre of the business district at Cabot Square, where belowground are miles of shops. Bear left at the end of West India Avenue onto Wren Landing and across North Dock Footbridge to reach the ❿ WEST INDIA DOCKS for one last dose of history. For this was one of the busiest ports in the world, importing all manner of things: sugar, rum, teak, mahogany,

Opposite: The Grapes public house, Narrow Street

coffee. The ⑪ BROWNS BUILDING, ahead of you, was a sugar warehouse built in the early 19th century by Napoleonic prisoners of war. The ⑫ MUSEUM OF LONDON DOCKLANDS is a few doors down, if you're curious to learn more. From here, the nearest DLR Station is at West India Quay, 100 metres east of the footbridge.

STARTING POINT
Tower Hill Underground Station

GETTING THERE
District & Circle Line

① THE DICKENS INN
Marble Quay, St Katharine's Way
London E1W 1UH
+44 20 7488 2208
www.dickensinn.co.uk

② PIER HEAD
St Katharine's & Wapping
London E1W 1PN

③ WAPPING OLD STAIRS
Next to the Town of Ransgate pub:
62 Wapping High Street
London E1W 2PN

④ TOBACCO DOCK
Tobacco Quay, Wapping Lane
London E1W 2SF
+44 20 7680 4001
www.tobaccodocklondon.com

⑤ SHADWELL BASIN
St Katharine's & Wapping
London E1W 3TD

⑥ THE PROSPECT OF WHITBY
57 Wapping Wall, London E1W 3SH
+44 20 7481 1095
www.taylor-walker.co.uk

⑦ WAPPING HYDRAULIC POWER STATION
25 Wapping Wall, London E1W 3SF

⑧ THE NARROW
44 Narrow Street, London E14 8DP
+44 20 7592 7950
www.gordonramsayrestaurants.com

⑨ THE GRAPES
76 Narrow Street, London E14 8BP

⑩ WEST INDIA DOCKS
Canary Wharf, London E14

⑪ BROWNS BUILDING
West India Quay, Hertsmere Road
London E14 4ED

⑫ MUSEUM OF LONDON DOCKLANDS
No.1 Warehouse
West India Quay, Hertsmere Road
London E14 4AL
+44 20 7001 9844
www.museumoflondon.org.uk

Above: St Katharine's Way

Above: The skyscraper of Canary Wharf across the River Thames; Below: Brussels Wharf, Shadwell Basin

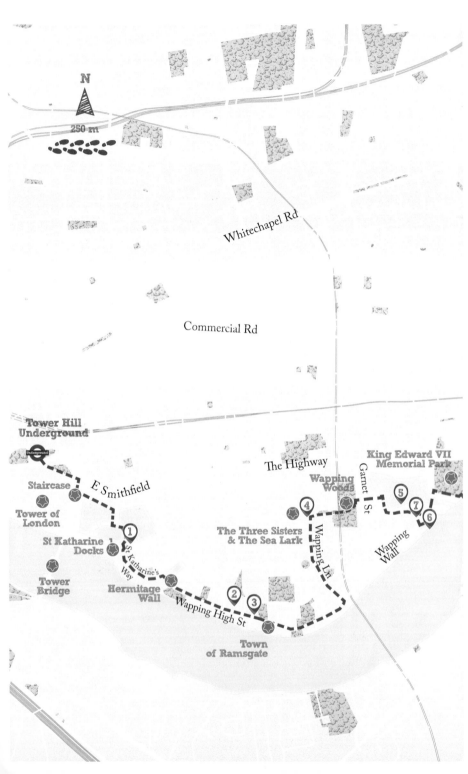

N

250 m

Whitechapel Rd

Commercial Rd

Tower Hill
Underground

The Highway

King Edward VII
Memorial Park

Staircase

E Smithfield

Wapping
Woods

Garnet St

⑤

Tower of
London

①

Wapping Ln

④

⑦
⑥

St Katharine
Docks

St Katharine's Way

The Three Sisters
& The Sea Lark

Wapping
Wall

Tower
Bridge

Hermitage
Wall

Wapping High St

②
③

Town
of Ramsgate

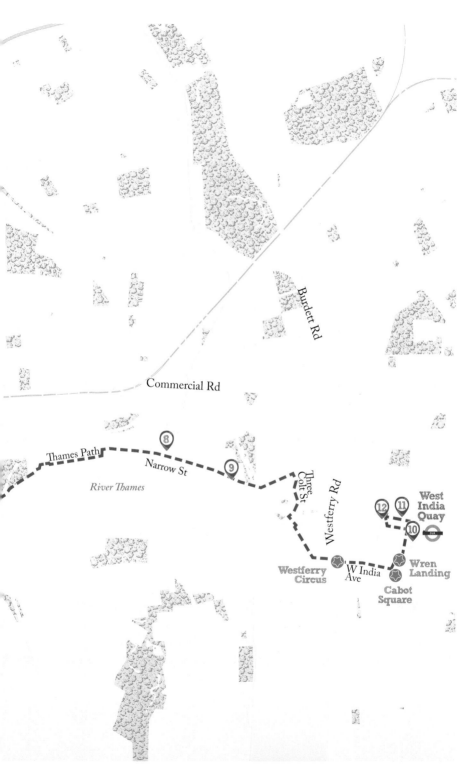

Burdett Rd

Commercial Rd

Thames Path

⑧

Narrow St

⑨

River Thames

Three Colt St

Westferry Rd

⑫ ⑪

West India Quay

⑩

Westferry Circus

W India Ave

Wren Landing

Cabot Square

18   The Artful Lunchtime Walk

The City of London

BEST TIME: For City workers, during lunch break; otherwise, a weekend when the City is deserted
DISTANCE: Approximately 4 kilometres

There is London, the capital of England, and then there is the City of London, which is a district within London that originally lay inside the ancient city walls. Colloquially known as the Square Mile (after its approximate size), the area has long-running links with trade and banking dating as far back as the Anglo-Saxon period. Whilst Greater London has spread laterally, the City has grown vertically, with skyscrapers galore, making it the most corporate of all London's boroughs.

Whether you're a local or experiencing the City of London for the first time, it's easy to lose perspective on what you want out of all this busy-ness. So, being able to step away for a moment and shelter in a chapel, secluded courtyard, or medieval ruin can be a real gift. For when you're in the thick of it, you can forget that there is beauty and artfulness all around. Look on this walk as an opportunity to view the City close up, taking a magnifying glass to the objects that others pass by every day, unseen. Wander down such atmospherically named passages as Austin Friars (once the location of a medieval friary) and St Swithin's Lane, and discover that while the City can overwhelm, with its maelstrom of traffic and building works, it can also offer comfort by enveloping you in its folds.

Step off the escalator at Liverpool Street Station and you'll find yourself in the shadow of the City's monoliths. Midweek, the fury of the fast-moving foot traffic can fire you up one moment and drain

Opposite: The Shard

you the next. Turn right on Bishopsgate, and keeping station-side, walk past the buses and heavy goods vehicles and turn into the rather modest grounds of ❶ ST BOTOLPH'S for sanctuary. Get up close and you'll see tucked into the chapel's alcoves two statuettes on either side of the main door; one a young boy with cap clasped in hand, the other a young girl.

Moving along the church path, you'll come across the most delightful incongruity. See it? The small domed building, with its countless mosaic tiles hand-pressed to its rounded body. This was once a ❷ TURKISH BATHHOUSE servicing 19th-century gentlemen.

Scoot through the gap between the office buildings towering ahead, turn left on Old Broad Street, and take the first right at the busy dual carriageway, onto London Wall. Aptly named, it is a road in the City of London running along part of the old defensive wall first constructed by the Romans to protect the ancient settlement of Londonium. Whilst the church you see here today – ❸ ALL HALLOWS-ON-THE-WALL – is a mere 250 years old, there has been a church on this site since the 12th century. It was the original church's proximity to the wall that protected it from the Great Fire in the 17th century. Across from the church is a small passageway next to an office building, home to Deutsche Bank. That's where you'll head next.

Eschewing modernity for solitude, press your hands to the cool brick buildings as you make your way, single-file, along the narrow passageway that is Austin Friars, via Great Winchester Street, and across to Adams Court. Here, space opens up as you step into the cloistered gardens of ❹ GIBSON HALL , with its neoclassical colonnade walk, tucked in back of one of the more congested inter-sections in London, where Threadneedle Street meets Bishopsgate.

Turn left on Bishopsgate and brace yourself for wall-to-wall buildings and traffic. How many City workers, I wonder, have sought

Opposite Victorian Turkish Bathhouse, Bishopsgate

respite in the secret courtyard garden of ❸ ST ETHELBURGA, one of those rare medieval churches to survive the Great Fire? In an unexpected twist, the caretakers have seen fit to erect a Bedouin tent where locals can come to meditate during their lunch break.

For a startling juxtaposition of contrasts, turn back and retrace your steps along Bisopsgate until you come to Great St Helen's. Turn left, and then left again onto Undershaft, where the elongated dome of one of the city's most distinctive skyscrapers, ❼ ST MARY AXE (THE GHERKIN), designed by renowned architect Sir Norman Foster, soars above the spared medieval church, ❽ ST HELEN'S BISHOPSGATE.

Pause often along this walk through the City, taking in your immediate vicinity; look up and far ahead into the distance, and you'll encounter artful objects, some no higher than your knee and others rising many storeys into the sky.

Situated across the street from the Gherkin is a seven-metre sculpture of a cartoon-style girl clutching a teddy bear. This impressive sculpture, titled *Charity*, is the work of prominent Brit artist Damien Hirst. Turn right onto St Mary Axe and stand at the junction with Leadenhall Street, where the buildings themselves morph into sculptures as you look across the road to ❾ LLOYD'S OF LONDON and gaze up and up at ❿ THE LEADENHALL BUILDING, which reaches to the clouds, its shape suggesting an elongated pyramid.

Continue on to Lime Street; at the end turn left on Fenchurch Street and then right on Rood Lane, which merges into St Mary at Hill. Here, you'll catch first sight of the Shard south of the river before turning left on St Dunstan's Lane and straying into the medieval ruins of ⓫ ST DUNSTAN-IN-THE-EAST. There's something very special about this romantically timeworn place, nestled amidst 21st-century builds, with its wild garden growing robustly within the old stone remains. Those seeking a peaceful place to eat lunch or steal a few quiet moments – City workers and tourists alike – can find refuge here.

The Cheesegrater building, amongst others; St Bortolph's; City office building; St Dunstan-in-the-East; City of London bench; St Mary Axe (The Gherkin)

From St Dunstan's, head west along Lower Thames Street and come off at Monument Street, where you'll begin to follow a trail of objects with historical significance, both large and small, in plain view and concealed. The first, a grand Doric column in the classical tradition, can be found at the junction of Monument Street and Fish Street Hill. Erected between 1671 and 1677, ⑪ THE MONUMENT commemorates the Great Fire of London and celebrates the rebuilding of the City. Inside is a spiral cantilevered stone staircase comprising 311 steps leading to a viewing platform. Originally, the Monument was surmounted by a drum and a copper urn from which flames emerged, symbolizing the Great Fire.

Carry on to the end of Monument Street, and turn right up King William Street and left onto Cannon Street at Monument Station. You're heading for No. 111 (keep an eye out for Boots chemist opposite), where the next article is low to the ground, sealed off by an iron grill. It may not look very remarkable, but this irregular piece of limestone is the remnant of a much larger block that stood for many centuries on the south side of the street. The name ⑫ LONDON STONE was first recorded around the year 1100. Possibly of Roman origin, there has been interest and speculation about it since at least the 16th century, with claims that it was a focus of veneration, or has some occult significance.

Turn up neighbouring St Swithin's Lane, take a left along the passageway marked Mansion House Place, and another left onto St Stephen's Row. This series of courts and alleyways preserves the spirit of the Restoration period as well as another significant Christopher Wren monument: ⑬ ST STEPHEN WALBROOK. Wander through Walbrook's sheltered churchyard before stepping inside this 340-year-old church for a transcendent moment. Admire its lofty Byzantine domed interior and imagine the smell of burning incense and angelic voices singing out Mass; then walk back out into daylight and towards the axis of the City, Bank Station.

Opposite: Leadenhall Market on Gracechurch Street

Left: St Margaret Pattens Church
and the Walkie Talkie Building on
Fenchurch Street

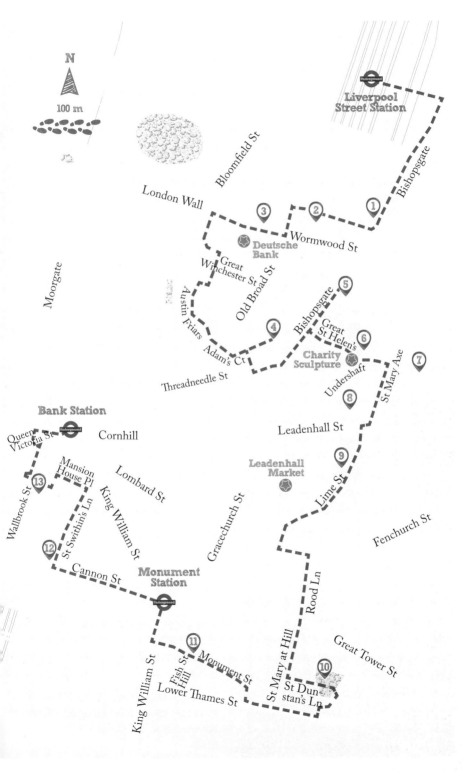

19__ The After-Dark Walk
Clerkenwell

BEST TIME: Around dusk
DISTANCE: Approximately 2.5 kilometres

Some places in London are more atmospheric *after* the sun goes down. If you enjoy being a little spooked, I recommend setting off on your Clerkenwell walk late on a winter's afternoon as the skies are darkening. Be sure to take a friend, and probably best not to read up on the area's ancient history of body snatching, bloodshed, and murder beforehand if you're aiming to venture very far.

From Farringdon Station, turn left out of the exit and left again onto Turnmill Street, which runs parallel to the train tracks. Take the first right, on Benjamin Street, and left on Britton Street. At the end of the second block, you'll pass ❶ THE JERUSALEM TAVERN, whose roots reach back to the Crusades. Dare to go down St John's Path, which runs alongside the pub, and instantly you are caught up in Clerkenwell's capillary of alleyways. As city workers revel after-hours only a street away, you could wander for long stretches without encountering another soul. At the medieval ❷ ST JOHN'S GATE, to the right of the path's end, you'll find yourself standing beneath one of the few tangible remnants of Clerkenwell's monastic past; from here, during the Crusades, Hospitaller Knights of the Order of St John would set out for the Holy Land to tend to pilgrims.

Bear left, crossing the busy A5201 (Clerkenwell Road), and the 21st century's intrusion on this medieval complex is abundantly apparent in St John's Square with its gentrification and modernisations; but there's something to be said for the dazzling contrast between the old and new. Here, in the centre of what was once the watchmaking community, graphic designers mill around a complex of Georgian town houses and warehouses-cum-boutique hotels. Get here

Opposite: St John's Gate

Clockwise from top left: **Priory Church of Saint Bartholomew the Great; The Jerusalem Tavern; St John's Path; St John's Square; Charterhouse**

whilst it is still light, and you can wander through the ❸ PRIORY CHURCH OF THE ORDER OF ST JOHN to the beautiful secret garden in back. Beneath the chapel is an early English crypt, a rare find in this darkly becoming corner of London. Cross the courtyard and step inside ❹ THE ZETTER TOWNHOUSE for a hedonistic moment of excess, where you'll find a hotel lobby stuffed to bursting with all manner of lamps, Queen Anne-style furniture, and a menagerie of taxidermy.

Hedonism and monasticism have always been bedfellows in Clerkenwell. Nearby Charterhouse had four taverns just outside the monastery walls. Hidden alongside the Zetter Townhouse, you'll find Jerusalem Passage, the original location of the Jerusalem Tavern. The blasting through of Clerkenwell Road in 1878 wrecked the ancient geography of this section of London, but Jerusalem Passage survived. At the end of the passageway, turn right on Aylesbury Street, right on St John Street, and then, if it feels safe to do so, slip down the modern walkway of Brewery Square and turn right on Northburgh Street. On the corner of Great Sutton Street, ❺ THE SLAUGHTERED LAMB has punters queuing two deep for the bar and hosts popular music gigs in its snug cellar space. Allusions to the area's Masonic past turn up here in the form of a red neon pentagram as the stage backdrop. A block east, ❻ THE SUTTON ARMS on the junction with Berry Street is a no-frills, quaint, old-fashioned pub, which is larger on the inside than it looks from the exterior.

Head south down Berry Street back to Clerkenwell Road. Turn right and keep walking until you reach the intersection with St John Street. Along the way, you will see the wall marking the boundary of Charterhouse Precincts, a 14th-century Carthusian monastery, whose Tudor and later buildings occupy a sizeable piece of land in the heart of Clerkenwell. Few people ever get to see inside the complex, making it something of an enigma to the uninitiated. Turn left down St John Street and continue to Charterhouse Street, and ❼ SMITHFIELD MARKET – a sight to behold.

Before the market, though, I urge you to turn left onto Charter-house Street and take the left fork up to the locked iron gates at the southern end of the Precincts. Peering through the bars, you can see directly through to the almshhouse and former monastery that is the ❽ CHARTERHOUSE. Given the darkness and the sinister gated threshold, you may well feel a chill go down your spine.

Retrace your steps to Smithfield. The market itself is an airy space by Sir Horace Jones, who also designed Leadenhall Market in the City and Tower Bridge. The two main buildings of this Grade II-listed complex are joined by Grand Avenue, a central shopping arcade. Jones covered the structure with great, open iron-trussed roofs to admit natural light and air. It's hard to credit that this is London's oldest surviving meat market. Imagine the scene a few hundred years ago: the ground covered with filth and mire, and the mayhem of cattle bellowing and squealing as they were herded into the slaughter. The party street you see fronting Smithfield today is a far cry from what came before. The market hall is built on the site of the notorious St Bartholomew's Fair, where witches were burned at the stake and revolutionaries, including Scottish freedom fighter William Wallace, were executed.

Walk around to West Smithfield in back, and you are now crossing paths with the old Victorian body snatchers, who would regularly produce warm cadavers for unethical anatomists at St Bartholomew's Hospital. The truly curious might like to come back and visit the rather macabre ❾ BART'S PATHOLOGY MUSEUM (amongst the hospital buildings) in the daytime, which stores the skull of John Bellingham – the only person to assassinate a British prime minister.

At the roundabout behind Smithfield market, cross over to Cloth Fair. The fate of these alleys becomes more precious and precarious by the day. Buried deep in the back streets, you'll find London's oldest surviving church, the ❿ PRIORY CHURCH OF SAINT BARTHOLOMEW THE GREAT. Incredible to think that close to 900 years ago, friars came and went from this Augustinian

Above: The clock and decorative ironwork in Smithfield Market

priory, pacing along these same passageways. Opposite, you'll find the
⓫ RISING SUN tavern. Legend has it that in the 19th century, a
gang of body snatchers would drink here, with the odd regular known
to go missing, never to be seen again. On that menacing note, take
the next left and head right on East Passage via the ⓬ OLD RED
COW pub before turning up Cloth Street and along Long Lane into
the safe hands of London Public Transport at the Barbican.

Above: The Rising Sun pub
on Cloth Fair

STARTING POINT
Farringdon Underground Station

GETTING THERE
Metropolitan, Circle, or
Hammersmith & City Lines

1 THE JERUSALEM TAVERN
55 Britton Street
London EC1M 5UQ
+44 20 7490 4281
www.stpetersbrewery.co.uk

2 ST JOHN'S GATE
St John's Lane, London EC1M 4DA

3 PRIORY CHURCH OF THE ORDER OF ST JOHN
Clerkenwell, London EC1V 4JJ
+44 20 7324 4005
www.museumstjohn.org.uk

4 THE ZETTER TOWNHOUSE
49–50 St John's Square
London EC1V 4JJ
+44 20 7324 4005
www.thezettertownhouse.com

5 THE SLAUGHTERED LAMB
34–35 Great Sutton Street
London EC1V 0DX
+44 20 7253 1516
www.theslaughteredlambpub.com

6 THE SUTTON ARMS
16 Great Sutton Street
London EC1V 0DH
+44 20 7253 2462

7 SMITHFIELD MARKET
Charterhouse Street
London EC1A 9PQ
+44 20 7248 3151
www.smithfieldmarket.com

8 CHARTERHOUSE
Charterhouse Square
London EC1M 6AN
+44 20 7 253 9503
www.thecharterhouse.org

9 BART'S PATHOLOGY MUSEUM
Robin Brook Centre, 3rd Floor
West Smithfield
London EC1A 7BE
+44 20 7882 5555
www.smd.qmul.ac.uk

10 PRIORY CHURCH OF ST BARTHOLOMEW THE GREAT
Cloth Fair, London EC1A 7JQ
+44 20 7600 0440
www.greatstbarts.com

11 RISING SUN
38 Cloth Fair
London EC1A 7JQ
+44 20 7726 6671
www.risingsunbarbican.co.uk

12 OLD RED COW
71–72 Long Lane
London EC1A 9EJ
+44 20 7726 2595
www.theoldredcow.com

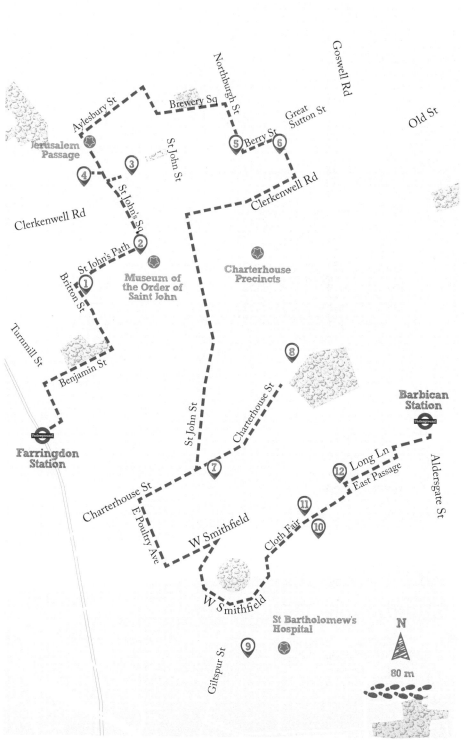

20__ The East End Market Lovers' Walk

Dalston to Hackney to Hoxton

BEST TIME: Saturday
DISTANCE: Approximately 5 kilometres

Hackney has hosted the liveliest East End street markets for centuries, and there are no signs of their popularity abating. This walk takes in three of its oldest and most resilient markets, as well as the community's roots (a mixture of Afro-Caribbean, Asian, and European middle and working classes), whose contributions, over generations, have welded a vibrant and enduring sense of both unity and individual identity. Step out at Dalston Kingsland BR Station, and you're greeted by the energetic bursts of African drums and reggae, the sounds of traders, and dance music floating in the air from across the street at ❶ RIDLEY ROAD MARKET. Going strong since the 1880s, this market has sold fruit, vegetables, and a wide range of household goods to generations of families.

Stretching as far as St Mark's Rise, this locals' market may not be high up there on tourists' hit lists of fashionable London shopping destinations, but it unaffectedly offers up the *real* East End experience. Continue past the costermongers selling exotic produce, the colourful fabric stalls, and Turkish supermarket, all the way down Riley Road to Dalston Lane, which remains a hub for music and nightlife thanks to the community's laid-back attitude. For a time, all-night warehouse and house parties were the rage around here. The legendary Four Aces Club, which closed down in 1997, was situated farther back on Dalston Lane, underneath what is now the CLR James Library. The venue started life as a vaudeville theatre and picture palace (common to the area), before being turned into a music

Opposite: Ridley Road Market stall

216

Clockwise from top left: Wilton Way; street art; Market Café, Broadway Market; Climpson & Son; Cat & Mutton; Hackney Empire Building

spot in 1966. Celebrating the best of Afro-Caribbean music, the club was a destination for the whole Dalston community and remained a favourite among musicians as well, with Bob Marley, Bob Dylan, and Chrissie Hynde all performing there.

About 300 metres along Dalston Lane, keep an eye out for ❷ NAVARINO MANSIONS, the elaborately designed mansion block with plaster architraves, relief plaques, and curved railings. A central entrance to the site has the building name on an ornate stucco band above a row of three archways. Built in 1905 by a philanthropic association, the residences were originally intended to accommodate 300 Jewish artisans from the East End. Turning onto Navarino Road, alongside the mansions, you'll see why the area began attracting teachers and doctors, bohemians and dropouts, in the 1980s and '90s: its fantastic stock of cheap (at the time) Georgian and Victorian houses.

Take the third turning on your left, onto Wilton Way, and you've hit the off-the-beaten-track jackpot. At first, this cluster of traditional shopfronts with old-fashioned lettering looks incredibly dated, but inside, these independent businesses are anything but old hat. Take ❸ WILTON WAY CAFE, which not only caters to a steady stream of 20- to 30-somethings but is also home to London Fields Radio, which interviews guests in a tiny corner of the cafe. Keeping things in the community, the cafe sources their coffee beans from nearby Climpson & Sons. If you're a history buff, you'll love quality household items store ❹ J GLINERT for its collection of pamphlets and books on London's East End. I could go on but there are simply too many wonderful places along this stretch to list.

Turn right off Wilton Way onto Eleanor Road and then take a left at Reading Lane. At the end of the street, you'll come out at a main square that houses not one but three landmark buildings: ❺ HACKNEY TOWN HALL, ❻ HACKNEY EMPIRE and ❼ HACKNEY PICTUREHOUSE. Hackney Empire is a legendary London music hall where Charlie Chaplin and Stan Laurel trod the boards during the venue's heyday. Iconic in many Londoners' minds, the giant 3-D logo at the top of the building makes me want to cheer this borough for remaining so staunchly committed to its roots.

Next up is our second East End market, and also its most fashionable and popular: ⓫ BROADWAY MARKET. To get there, head to London Fields, a small common, via Martello Street (off Reading Lane, by the side of the Town Hall), where you can enjoy sitting outside with a pint at ⓼ PUB ON THE PARK or rummaging through the second-hand lot under the arches. Keep walking south across the Fields, until you come out at the ⓽ CAT & MUTTON on the corner of the market. Downstairs, it's a traditional pub with comfy mismatched furniture, retro mirrors, and old ceiling features made of tin. Upstairs, by way of a spiral staircase, is Pearl's cocktail lounge: a crepuscular bar with creative drinks, heavily draped windows, and panoramic views of the market below.

Saturday mornings, along Broadway, you'll find dozens of stalls selling cheese, meat, fish, pastries, and preserves. While you can spend hours pecking around the various stands, hoarding goodies to take away, you may be tempted to go inside to eat, especially if you look in the window at ⓾ SARAY BROADWAY CAFÉ and see the Turkish lady industriously rolling out two-foot-wide crepes and packing them with all manner of delicious fillings. More of an Aladdin's cave inside, with its own fish pond at the back, it's a snug place to squirrel away and tuck into mezze. Those after a stronger tipple than tea might venture to ask for their *raki*.

Moving down Broadway, away from London Fields, you'll see new designer shops rubbing shoulders seamlessly with long-standing stalwarts. There's Percy Ingle's Bakery alongside newcomer Hill & Szrok butchers; the betting shop next door to Buggies & Bikes; and F Cooke pie and mash neighbouring the design studio Fabrications. There go, also, those unmistakeably East London millennials – young sartorial men with handlebar moustaches or Stonewall Jacksons, parading around.

Clockwise from top left: Saray Broadway Café; Hackney Empire; Broadway Market street sign; Cat & Mutton public house; fish stall; Pub on the Park

Cross over the canal bridge onto Goldsmiths' Row, and after about 500 metres, look out for a gate near the end of the Row. Wandering down this little side path, the last thing you'd expect to find is an attractive cafe positioned alongside a yard stabling livestock, the home of ⓬ HACKNEY CITY FARM. For Brits of a certain age, the whole endeavour brings back memories of a popular sitcom called *The Good Life*, about a couple named Dan and Barbara who escape the rat race by converting their garden into a farm and becoming totally self-sufficient.

Cut through to the west side of Haggeston Park and exit to the left on Queensbridge Road. Take the first right, on Dunloe Street, and continue all the way down Dunloe until you reach the back of a very interesting-looking building. Walk around the block onto Kingsland Road, and peering through the railings, you'll see an attractive row of dark brick 18th-century almshouses set around a leafy courtyard, resplendent with planted London plane trees. For the longest time, I'd been hearing about this place: a museum in London where you can step back into the past, wandering through a series of period rooms, experiencing how home life would have been for an Edwardian, Georgian, or Victorian family. The notion of immersion in the finery and ambience of another era, another life, appealed to my sensibilities. From my very first glimpse of the ⓭ GEFFRYE MUSEUM's exterior, I was smitten. My pleasure only doubled when I learned there were also period gardens open from spring into autumn.

Coming out of the museum onto Kingsland Road, turn right and take the first left, down Hare Walk, crossing Stanway and continuing through to Tyssen Street before making a left on Hoxton Street and arriving at the ⓮ HOXTON STREET MARKET.

Minutes away from the City and brimming with locals, especially on a Saturday, this place is rich in history. Established in 1687, Hoxton is the oldest street market in Hackney. Some fine Victorian

Opposite: Geffrye Museum

storefronts remain, together with some listed buildings. This once-thriving market was long the cornerstone of the community but, with the proliferation of supermarkets, began to struggle. In recent years, the council and neighbourhood businesses have been working together to revive the market, including the introduction of new shops.

Make your way along Hoxton Street to No. 130. From outside, the Grade-II listed building doesn't look like very much, but ⓯ HOXTON HALL is a prime example of a saloon-style Victorian music hall dating back to 1863; for this whole area was once the longtime playground to London's aristocracy and working classes, rivalling the West End for entertainment. Recently, the venue has experienced something of a renaissance after receiving some major investment and undergoing significant restoration which was completed in 2015. You may want to check it out from the inside.

A joyous new addition to the neighbourhood is ⓰ HOXTON STREET MONSTER SUPPLIES & MINISTRY OF STORIES, further down on your right, at No. 159. In front, it purports to be a "Purveyor of Quality Goods for Monsters of Every Kind," selling "Bespoke and Everyday Items for the Living, Dead or Undead." In back, it is the London equivalent to 826 Valencia in San Francisco, which runs engaging writing programs for local school-children.

This street is where Hackney natives come to do their grocery shopping, hunt for bargains, and visit the local library. The atmosphere is relaxed and friendly, no matter the time of day. When you're all walked out, take the next left, on Falkirk Street, crossing Kingsland Road and continuing on to Cremer Street, where Hoxton BR Station is located, behind the Geffrye Museum.

Above: Hoxton Street Market sign; Below: Market fruit stall

1 RIDLEY ROAD MARKET
Ridley Road, London E8
+44 20 3189 1970
www.ridleyroad.co.uk

2 NAVARINO MANSIONS
234 Dalston Lane, London E8 1LB
+44 20 7923 0745
www.ids.org.uk

3 WILTON WAY CAFE
63 Wilton Way, London E8 1BG
www.londonfieldsradio.co.uk/the-cafe

4 J GLINERT
71 Wilton Way, London E8 1BS
+44 20 7249 6815
www.jglinert.com

5 HACKNEY TOWN HALL
Mare Street, London E8 1EA
+44 20 8356 3000
www.hackney.gov.uk

6 HACKNEY EMPIRE
291 Mare Street, London E8 1EJ
+44 20 8985 2424
www.hackneyempire.co.uk

7 HACKNEY PICTUREHOUSE
270 Mare Street, London E8 1HE
+44 871 902 5734
www.picturehouses.co.uk

8 PUB ON THE PARK
19 Martello Street, London E8 3PE
+44 20 7923 3398
www.pubonthepark.com

9 CAT & MUTTON
76 Broadway Market, London E8 4QJ
+44 20 7249 6555
www.catandmutton.co.uk

10 SARAY BROADWAY CAFÉ
58 Broadway Market, London E8 4QJ
+44 20 7684 1651

11 BROADWAY MARKET
Hackney, London E8 4QJ
+44 7872 463409
www.broadwaymarket.co.uk

12 HACKNEY CITY FARM
1a Goldsmiths Row, London E2 8QA
+44 20 7729 6381
www.hackneycityfarm.co.uk

13 GEFFRYE MUSEUM
136 Kingsland Road, London E2 8EA
+44 20 7739 9893
www.geffrye-museum.org.uk

14 HOXTON STREET MARKET
Hoxton Street, London N1
www.hackney.gov.uk/hoxton-market

15 HOXTON HALL
130 Hoxton Street, London N1 6SH
+44 20 7684 0060
www.hoxtonhall.co.uk

16 HOXTON STREET
MONSTER SUPPLIES & MINISTRY
OF STORIES
159 Hoxton Street, London N1 6PJ
+44 20 7729 4159
www.ministryofstories.org
www.monstersupplies.org

21__ The Time On Your Hands Walk

Blackheath to Greenwich

BEST TIME: Saturday, for Greenwich Market
DISTANCE: Approximately 6 kilometres

Stepping out of Blackheath BR Station into this picturesque village, you're well away from the tourist trail. It's a lovely place for residents to potter, with a farmers' market on Sundays, excellent neighbourhood bistros like Locale for Italian fare and Buenos Aires Café, a homey-looking place on the edge of the Heath, and a great local pub called the Hare & Billet tucked away on Hare & Billet Road. From the station, bear left onto Tranquil Vale (which later turns into Goffers Road) until you reach the Heath; then join the path heading east toward the church.

At ❶ ALL SAINTS CHURCH, follow the bend in the footpath around, keeping Goffers Road parallel. Stomp freely across 200 acres of parkland – the site of the old plague pits where the dead bodies of the afflicted were dumped in the 17th century – whilst admiring the ring of splendid Georgian town houses bordering the horizon. It's hard to believe you are in Zone 3 of London when you are treated to such an expanse of sky and space.

Then it dawns on you. No building is higher than the spire on All Saints Church; there's not a skyscraper or a tower block in sight. How is that possible? Remarkably, it transpires that some influential locals had it written into law – a century or so ago – that no resident's view can be obstructed. That law still stands today. You realise how monumental this is when you later gaze out from the summit of the Royal Observatory in Greenwich and witness the limitless race to colonise East London with a clustering of skyscrapers and an expanse of towering new builds.

Opposite: View from on high in Greenwich Park

Above: All Saints Church, Blackheath; Below: View of Queen's House from Greenwich Park

On Blackheath, though, one feels curiously abroad *from* London. Here, you'll see families indulging their holiday fantasies with donkey rides up by the park and enjoying ice-cream cones bought from vendors who park up their vans even in deepest winter.

Pass through the gates ahead and leave the Heath for the more groomed grounds of Greenwich Park by way of tree-lined Blackheath Avenue. Past Charlton Way and the cricket patch, a path on your left leads to the ❷ RANGER'S HOUSE, a medium-sized redbrick Georgian mansion in the Palladian style. Home to the exceptional fine and decorative arts collection of diamond magnate Sir Julius Wernher (1850–1912), it is a pleasure to explore.

Returning to Blackheath Avenue, you'll soon arrive at the ❸ ROYAL OBSERVATORY GREENWICH. Situated on a hill, the observatory has played a major role in the history of astronomy and navigation since 1675, and is best known as the location of the prime meridian, meaning the location of every place on Earth is expressed in terms of its distance east or west from this line. Here, clusters of visitors pause to take in the panoramic view: the town's landmarks descending like a layer cake down to the banks of the River Thames. Straddling the meridian line, you'll have a foot in each hemisphere. Not bad for a short stroll.

Down the hill, head for the building at the midpoint of the neoclassical colonnades. This is ❹ QUEEN'S HOUSE. The story goes that James I gifted the house to his wife, Anne of Denmark, by way of apology for swearing in front of her after she accidentally killed one of his favourite dogs during a hunt. Sadly, Anne died in 1619, before the home was completed, but work resumed in 1629, when James's son Charles I gave the whole of Greenwich to his wife Henrietta Maria. There are no records of what he might have been apologizing for.

Peering through the colonnades from the east wing of Queen's House, you are afforded one of the finest views in London. Ahead, a formal green lawn stretches towards the classical buildings that collectively form the ❺ OLD ROYAL NAVAL COLLEGE.

Between the college's buildings you can see the River Thames and, beyond, the shimmering skyscrapers of Canary Wharf. Rather than walk straight to the college though, you'll find the older parts of the town are well worth wandering around.

Take the path bordering the park that connects Queen's House and the National Maritime Museum until you come to King William Walk. Cross the street towards the Greenwich Tavern, which is well positioned for views of the park and observatory. Continue along the architecturally handsome Nevada Street and you'll come across local hangout ❺ HEAP'S SAUSAGES. Next, turn right onto Stockwell Street and then take the first left and right to reach Roan Street, which leads around to St Alfege Passage. Look out for the original almshouses around ❻ ST ALFEGE CHURCH, which once provided homes for the poor and elderly of Greenwich.

At Church Street, take a left and cross the street, entering ❼ GREENWICH MARKET by way of Turnpin Lane or Durnford Street. Located within the original slaughterhouses for cattle and stables for horses, the covered bazaar is populated with 120 stalls set amidst shops. Come here for antiques and collectibles on Tuesdays, Thursdays, and Fridays; and craft and design on Wednesday, Fridays, Saturdays, and Sundays. Of all London's markets, this one is the makers' market, with local milliners, jewellery artists, and furniture designers basing their businesses here. While it can get rather crowded, it's a vibrant atmosphere with a London crowd. Hungry? Grab a bite to eat from one of the hot food vendors or try local favourite ❽ GODDARDS AT GREENWICH, accessed from King William Walk, for an authentic South London dining experience.

To explore the Naval College, walk north on King William Walk and enter via its grand avenue, College Way. The ❿ PAINTED HALL has been described as the "Sistine Chapel of the UK" and recognised as the greatest piece of decorative painting in England, whilst the ⓫ CHAPEL OF ST PETER AND ST PAUL is a neoclassical masterpiece and one of the country's finest 18th-century interiors. In

Clockwise from top left: **Queen's House** colonnades; **Royal Observatory Greenwich**; **Greenwich Market** entrance; inside Greenwich market; **Queen's House**; a rose-ringed parrot in Greenwich Park

the spaces between the hall and the chapel, you can gaze upon the crest on which Queen's House sits, and the observatory above.

Come out the East Gate of the campus, not far from the ⑫ TRAFALGAR TAVERN, on Park Row, where you'll lose sight of the river as you duck down the passageway at the back of the public house, respectfully saluting the statue of Nelson as you pass it by. Once on the Thames Path proper, with the river in view, two structures will come into sight: one a disused pier and the other the industrial defunct power station, both emblems of our maritime past. But what you won't see coming is ⑬ TRINITY HOSPITAL, until you are just steps away. This white, Gothic-style almshouse with its battlement façade has a distinct whimsicality, which is all the more enhanced by its boundary wall being pressed up against the Victorian power station next door. Rarely open to the public, access is granted during Open House weekend, usually in September.

Retracing your steps back to Nelson's statue, follow the Thames Path towards town, and there she is: the ⑭ CUTTY SARK. Like most schoolchildren in London, I was brought here on a class outing when I was young. I cannot recall what we were taught on that day, but I do remember vividly the fondness with which the ship was spoken about. One of the last tea clippers built, she was also one of the fastest. Today, she stands raised up proudly on the concourse, her three masts jutting up to rival the distant, towering Canary Wharf.

Just past the bow of the *Cutty Sark*, you'll see a small domed structure at the end of the concourse. What looks like a building the size of a public lavatory is in fact the entry point to the ⑮ GREENWICH FOOT TUNNEL, an underground walkway that leads beneath the River Thames to the Isle of Dogs, which stands in Canary Wharf's backyard.

I highly recommend returning and revisiting this walk again in the evening. If you set off from Blackheath at twilight, you'll arrive at the *Cutty Sark* at dusk, just in time to watch as the city's lights turn on.

Opposite: The *Cutty Sark*

STARTING POINT
Blackheath BR Station

GETTING THERE
Overground from Victoria or
London Bridge

1 ALL SAINTS CHURCH
All Saints Drive, London SE3 0TY
+44 20 8852 4280
www.allsaintsblackheath.org

2 THE RANGER'S HOUSE
(WERNHER COLLECTION)
Chesterfield Walk, London SE10 8QX
+44 20 8853 0035

3 ROYAL OBSERVATORY
GREENWICH
Blackheath Avenue, London SE10 8XJ
+44 20 8858 4422
www.rmg.co.uk/royal-observatory

4 QUEEN'S HOUSE
Romney Road
London SE10 9NF
+44 20 8858 4422
www.rmg.co.uk/queens-house

5 HEAP'S SAUSAGES
8 Nevada Street, London SE10 9JL
+44 20 8293 9199
www.heapssausages.com

6 ST ALFEGE CHURCH
Greenwich Church Street
London SE10 9BJ
+44 20 8853 0687
www.st-alfege.org

7 GREENWICH MARKET
Greenwich, London SE10 9HZ
+44 20 8269 5096
www.greenwichmarketlondon.com

8 GODDARDS AT
GREENWICH
22 King William Walk
London SE10 9HU
+44 20 8305 9612
www.pieshop.co.uk/
about-goddards-pies

9 OLD ROYAL NAVAL
COLLEGE
King William Walk
London SE10 9NN
+44 20 8269 4799
www.ornc.org

10 PAINTED HALL
College Way, London SE10 9NN
+44 20 8269 4747
www.ornc.org

11 THE CHAPEL OF ST PETER
AND ST PAUL
College Way, London SE10 9NN
+44 20 8269 4747
www.ornc.org

12 TRAFALGAR TAVERN
Park Row, London SE10 9NW
+44 20 8858 2909
www.trafalgartavern.co.uk

13 TRINITY HOSPITAL
Garden and Riverside Almshouses
Old Woolwich Road
London SE10 9AS
+44 20 7726 4991
www.mercers.co.uk

14 CUTTY SARK
King William Walk, London SE10 9HT
+44 20 8858 4422
www.rmg.co.uk

15 GREENWICH FOOT TUNNEL
King William Walk, London SE10 9HT

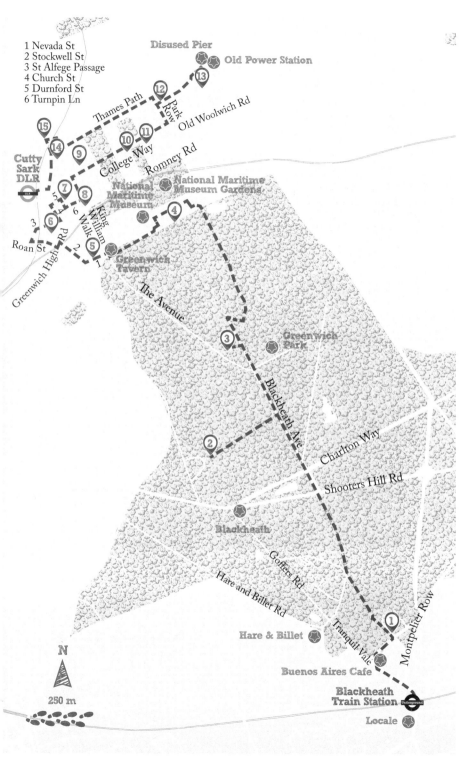

1 Nevada St
2 Stockwell St
3 St Alfege Passage
4 Church St
5 Durnford St
6 Turnpin Ln

Disused Pier

Old Power Station

13

12

Thames Path

Park Row

Old Woolwich Rd

15

14

9

10

11

College Way

Romney Rd

Cutty
Sark
DLR

7

8

National
Maritime
Museum

National Maritime
Museum Gardens

5

4

6

King William Walk

4

3

6

Roan St

2

5

Greenwich
Tavern

Greenwich High Rd

1

The Avenue

3

Greenwich
Park

Blackheath Ave

Charlton Way

Shooters Hill Rd

2

Blackheath

Goffers Rd

Hare and Billet Rd

Hare & Billet

Tranquil Vale

Montpelier Row

1

Buenos Aires Cafe

Blackheath
Train Station

Underground

Locale

N

250 m

22__ The Queen & Country Walk

Victoria to Chelsea

BEST TIME: May, leading up to Chelsea Flower Show
DISTANCE: Approximately 8 Kilometres

For many, Chelsea conjures up images of Sloane Rangers and fashionistas parading along the King's Road or Sloane Street, swinging their Louis Vuitton and Prada shopping bags. This *is* "Absolutely Fabulous" territory, after all. Go beyond the façade though, and one finds a loyally patriotic neighbourhood. For when the British back something, they do so to the hilt, be it their soldiers in wartime or betting on the horses on Grand National Day. Not even a well-formed azalea or a well-baked cake escapes such ostentatious treatment.

From Victoria Station, make your way to Ebury Street via Lower Belgrave Street off Buckingham Palace Road. Note the blue plaque at ❶ NO. 22B, where Ian Fleming lived from 1934 to 1945. ❷ NO. 42 also has a fascinating history; not only was it home to Alfred Lord Tennyson, but after the First World War, it also was the head office of the Soldiers Embroidery Industry, where disabled veterans found work. At the intersection with Elizabeth Street (where you'll return later), is ❸ TOMTOM COFFEE HOUSE (specialists in hand-rolled Cuban cigars) and, across the way, the pink-painted parlour of ❹ PEGGY PORSCHEN (a bespoke cake company). Continuing past the elegant Georgian houses, you would never guess how far back Ebury Street's history goes – it even receives a mention in the 1,000-year-old *Domesday Book*.

Eventually, the street opens up to leafy Orange Square, where you'll find chic residents breakfasting outside the ❺ DAYLESFORD cafe or dipping in and out of one of the neighbourhood's many high-

Opposite: Peggy Porschen cake shop window display

Clockwise from top left: Statue of a Chelsea Pension outside the Royal Hospital; Poule au Pot; statue of a young Mozart on Orange Square; Peggy Porschen; Crosby Hall, Cheyne Walk

end interior-design shops. French bistro ❻ LA POULE AU POT dominates the local scene, having served up foie gras and escargots to A-list celebrities and royals for more than 50 years. The glamour quotient is only enhanced by the tidbit that actors Terence Stamp and Michael Caine shared a flat in this area in the swinging sixties. The square also plays host to ❼ PIMLICO ROAD FARMERS' MARKET on Saturday mornings, with fresh fruit and veg delivered from Chegworth Valley, and seafood from the East Anglian coast. The market retains a very local, word-of-mouth vibe where everyone in the know is checking out whether "the mushroom man" is there that week.

From Orange Square, follow Pimlico Road west, which merges with Royal Hospital Road, and you're only a few hundred metres from the true heart of Chelsea: ❽ ROYAL HOSPITAL, a group of gorgeous 300-year-old buildings designed by Sir Christopher Wren during the reign of Charles II. Since 1692, the hospital has offered care and comradeship for British Army veterans, known as the Chelsea Pensioners, in recognition of their loyal service. Keep an eye out for these iconic local characters, attired decoratively and distinctively in bright scarlet tunics and cornice hats. The touching detail about the Chelsea Pensioners is that they have no dependents, often applying for residence upon having lost a partner and craving the camaraderie they experienced during their service. Thanks to the installation of en suite bathrooms in 2009, women can now be counted among their number. Book a veteran-led tour of this Grade I- and II-listed site in advance, and you'll have the gift of a truly entertaining, unique excursion. Afterwards, you can wander around the lovely grounds, especially ❾ RANELAGH GARDENS, which boasts more than 500 mature trees. This is an amazing wooded oasis in the centre of London – and it is open to the public at no cost. Come May, the grounds of the Royal Hospital are transformed into an Eden-esque landscape, featuring inspirational small gardens and vibrant horticultural displays for the world's most famous botanical fair: the RHS Chelsea Flower Show. Held at Chelsea since 1912, this is the garden design equivalent of Paris Fashion Week, and you need to book well in advance to gain entry.

Leaving the hospital grounds, carry on to the end of Royal Hospital Road until you pass the ⑪ CHELSEA PHYSIC GARDEN, which are the oldest botanic gardens in London, and a hidden paradise. Resuming your walk, turn onto Cheyne Walk, which has some of London's more prestigious addresses. Henry VIII's Manor House and Winchester House once dominated the riverside here, replaced later by these tall, elegant terrace houses. Come the 1960s, however, the neighbourhood's tranquillity was rocked by the arrival of Mick Jagger and Marianne Faithfull, at ⑫ NO. 48, and Keith Richards and Anita Pallenberg, at ⑩ NO. 3.

Along the section of Cheyne Walk between Battersea Bridge and Lots Road, you will find a succession of attractive ⑬ HOUSEBOATS moored on the river. A notable resident is Damien Hirst, bad boy of the British art world. Go check the barges out but then retrace your steps, as you're heading up Old Church Street next, to another time-honoured institution: the ⑭ CHELSEA ARTS CLUB. One can't predict what the façade of this white stucco building will look like from one visit to the next. Ever changing, it is treated as its members' personal canvas. Famous for their charity balls, which were banned from the Albert Hall owing to their notoriety for rowdiness and "promiscuous" behaviour, the organizers moved things behind closed doors, and it's rumoured the club keeps up its lavish, decadent traditions to this day.

Turn right on Fulham Road and carry on until you reach a confectionary of a building on the corner of Sloane Avenue. An eclectic mix of Art Nouveau, Art Deco, and geometrical classicism, ⑮ MICHELIN HOUSE is home to Terence Conran's retail space and first London restaurant, Bibendum, but was originally designed as the quirky headquarters of Michelin Tyres.

Walk down Sloane Avenue, and you'll have looped around to the King's Road (British fashion's most famous street). A left brings you to the Duke of York Square. Whilst this is newly home to the ⑯ SAATCHI GALLERY, and also a place where locals gather in

Clockwise from top left: Cheyne Walk;
Duke of York Square; Union Jack flags;
Cheyne Walk houseboat; Saatchi Gallery;
public sculpture by Allister Bowtell, Duke
of York Square

the summer to watch Wimbledon live on giant outdoor screens, those more au fait with the area will know this as the former British Army barracks, sold by the UK Ministry of Defence in 2000.

During the Chelsea Flower Show in May, the shops in and around Sloane Square, Sloane Street, and Duke of York Square decorate their fronts with plants and flowers for *Chelsea in Bloom*, which is rapidly becoming another flower-show institution. A selection of retailers, including designer brands, showcase glorious floral displays, hoping to win prizes and woo plant-loving patrons.

Tucked in back of Sloane Square, accessed via Sloane Street, is ⓚ CADOGAN HALL, home to the Royal Philharmonic Orchestra and, in the summer, the Proms' chamber music concerts. Heading east from the square along Cliveden Place, you move into Belgravia. You'll know you've arrived at Eaton Square when you spot the creamy, classic, three-bay-wide terraced houses surrounding a communal garden. This stately setting ranks as one of the most fashionable addresses in London. Followers of British TV drama may even recognize this as the square where Lady Rosamund Painswick from *Downton Abbey* resided or where the Bellamy family home in *Upstairs, Downstairs* was located.

Here, elegant Victorian Elizabeth Street in Belgravia is not as internationally known as nearby Sloane Street but is a sophisticated alternative for locals. Well-to-do residents can do everything from picking up their prescriptions at the chemist to waltzing away with designer party frocks from high-end fashion stores. When shoppers aren't buying, they're meeting with friends at stylish restaurants or cafes, such as Poilâne or Thomas Cubitt. With its wide, tree-lined pavements, this pocket of London has a vibrant village ambience that spills onto the street throughout the year, from an outdoor summer party in support of a military charity to Christmas festivities that transform the place into a winter shoppers' dream with market stalls, twinkling lights, circus performers, and even a flock of reindeer. You have to give it to the British: we know how to put on a show!

Opposite: Poilâne, Elizabeth Street

SOBACHA TEA
made from roasted
buckwheat. It has a wheaty
aroma, subtly nutty flavour
with a smooth texture.
It is rich in minerals
such as zinc, potassium.
Extremely high in fibre
and protein.

We also serve a delicious
italian hot chocolate!

TEA £2. HOT CHOCOLATE £2.20

DRINK + CROISSANT
OR PAIN AU CHOCOLAT
£3

STARTING POINT
Victoria Underground Station
GETTING THERE
Victoria and/or Circle Lines

❶ IAN FLEMING'S HOUSE
22B Ebury Street
London SW1W 0LU

❷ ALFRED LORD TENNYSON'S HOUSE
40–42 Ebury Street
London SW1W 0LZ

❸ TOMTOM COFFEE HOUSE
114 Ebury Street
London SW1W 9QD
+44 20 7730 1771
www.tomtom.co.uk/About/
AboutCoffee.aspx

❹ PEGGY PORSCHEN CAKES
116 Ebury Street
London SW1W 9QQ
+44 20 7730 1316
www.peggyporschen.com

❺ DAYLESFORD
44B Pimlico Road
London SW1W 8LP
+44 20 7881 8060
www.daylesford.com

❻ LA POULE AU POT
231 Ebury Street
London SW1W 8UT
+44 20 7730 7763
www.pouleaupot.co.uk

❼ PIMLICO FARMERS' MARKET
Orange Square, Pimlico Road
London SW1W 8NE
+44 20 7833 0338
www.lfm.org.uk

❽ ROYAL HOSPITAL CHELSEA
Royal Hospital Road
London SW3 4SR
+44 20 7881 5200
www.chelsea-pensioners.co.uk

Opposite: **Ebury Street**

❾ RANELAGH GARDENS
Royal Hospital Chelsea
London SW3 4SR
+44 20 7881 5305
www.chelsea-pensioners.co.uk

❿ KEITH RICHARDS'S HOUSE
3 Cheyne Walk
London SW3 5QZ

⓫ CHELSEA PHYSIC GARDEN
66 Royal Hospital Road
London SW3 4HS
+44 20 7352 5646
www.chelseaphysicgarden.co.uk

⓬ MICK JAGGER'S HOUSE
48 Cheyne Walk
London SW3 5TS

⓭ CHEYNE WALK HOUSEBOATS
Cheyne Walk
London SW10

⓮ CHELSEA ARTS CLUB
143 Old Church Street
London SW3 6EB
+44 20 7376 3311
www.chelseaartsclub.com

⓯ MICHELIN HOUSE
81 Fulham Road
London SW3 6RD
+44 20 7581 5817
www.bibendum.co.uk

⓰ SAATCHI GALLERY
Duke of York's HQ
King's Road
London SW3 4RY
+44 20 7811 3070
www.saatchigallery.com

⓱ CADOGAN HALL
5 Sloane Terrace
London SW1X 9DQ
+44 20 7730 4500
www.cadoganhall.com

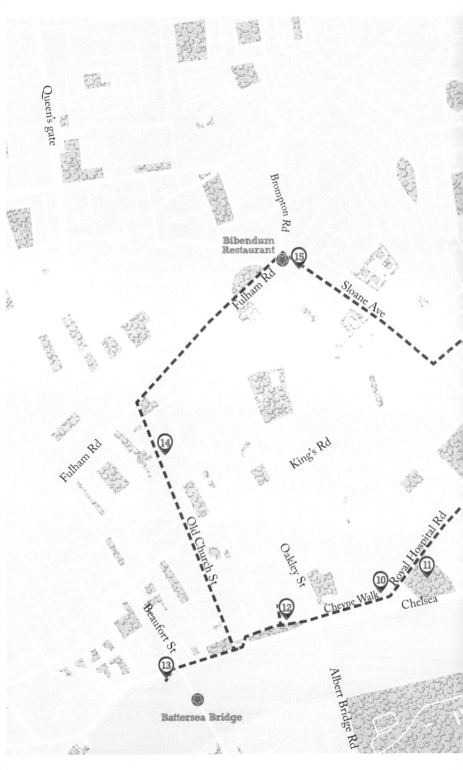

Belgrave Pl

Grosvenor
Gardens Exit

Eaton Square

①

②

Ebury St

Sloane St

Victoria
Station

Ⓤ Underground

⑰

Sedding St

Elizabeth St

Cliveden Pl

The Thomas
Cubitt

Poilâne

③

④

Buckingham Palace Rd

King's Rd

Sloane Square

⑤

The Duke
of York Square

⑦

⑥

Pimlico
Rd

⑯

Orange Square

Chelsea
Bridge Rd

East Rd

⑧

⑨

Embankment

N

250 m

The French Quarter Walk
Kensington

BEST TIME: Spring or summer
DISTANCE: Approximately 7 kilometres

London is home to several hundred thousand French nationals, with many calling Kensington home. French residents stroll through the surrounding mews or simply sit outside a cafe, reading *Le Monde*, wiping away crumbs from their morning croissants, or biting into baked baguettes. Wander around the neighbourhood and you'll overhear school-age children chattering away as they make their way to the local lycée, or Gallic-speaking families gathering for a matinee at the Ciné Lumière.

Turn right on Kensington High Street, and then take the first left down Young Street to escape the crowds and discover the gems locals like to keep to themselves. For that, your first stop must be Thackeray Street (first turning on your left, off Kensington Square Garden) and ❶ MONTPARNASSE CAFÉ. Here, you can play at being *trés Français* for a morning or afternoon, sipping a French press coffee and leafing through *Le Figaro* as you lean back, dreaming of Paris.

Circling around the French Embassy Cultural Department, located only a few streets away, you'll find some of Kensington's hidden byways – its charming mews. Turn right on Andsell Street and left on St Albans Grove to reach the ❷ BUILDERS ARMS, a gastropub housed in an attractive Georgian property usually filled with foreign students and ex-pats, particularly Americans studying at nearby Richmond University Kensington Campus. If you were to continue along Victoria Grove, you'd arrive at Gloucester Road and the restaurant L'etranger, where the service is *truly* Parisian (translation: indifferent and surly). Instead, head down Launceston Place, where you'll enter a series of maze-like mews, from ❸ KYNANCE

Opposite: Montparnasse Café

Clockwise from top left: Details of a statue in Kynance Mews; Kynance Mews; Kensington brims with many wonderful restaurants; Patisserie Valerie; Cornwall Mews West; a colorfully painted door in Kynance Mews

ALWAYS, at last arriving at the westernmost perimeter of this Kensington walk, which kisses the borders of Earl's Court Road. Here, you can taste classic Gallic dishes at the 4-star ② LITTLE FRENCH RESTAURANT on Hogarth Road, which is easy on both your taste buds and your purse. Even people who've lived here for years are bemused to stumble upon these gems.

Now, zoom across to South Kensington by way of Harrington Gardens. South Kensington is at the heart of French cultural life, with the Ciné Lumière, Lycée Français, and the French Institute all sharing a backyard between Queensberry and Cromwell Place and Cromwell and Harrington Roads.

If you thought Patisserie Valerie was tempting, wait until you peer through the polished window of ② AUX MERVEILLEUX DE FRED on Old Brompton Road. Here, the proprietors go to a whole other level to put on a show for passers-by; their bakers knead, roll, shape, and pipe South Kensington's creamiest, flakiest pastries in full view.

After a lazy Sunday lunch in the neighbourhood, residents stroll over to Queensberry Place for a screening at the ② CINÉ LUMIÈRE, which often projects French movie classics of the 1940s and 1950s.

Ending your love affair with French London at the lower end of Exhibition Road, wave goodbye to Paris and shades of Provence, and hello to Museum Mile.

This stretch of road distinguishes itself from other popular tourist destinations in the city by giving precedence to pedestrians over traffic – a rare luxury in London, so you may well want to savour it. Entire days could be spent here alone, visiting the ② NATURAL HISTORY MUSEUM, ② VICTORIA AND ALBERT MUSEUM, ② SCIENCE MUSEUM, and lesser-known ② ROYAL GEOGRAPHICAL SOCIETY.

While the cafe terraces on the pedestrianized precinct are reminiscent of Paris, this area is determinedly cosmopolitan. Puffa-

Above: Victoria and Albert Museum

jacketed Italians and fur-wearing Russians sip Americanos outside
❺ COMPTOIR LIBANAIS. All around, sophisticated eateries
and cafes vie for your patronage. If you do make it to the top of
Exhibition Road, it is worth cheekily asking the Royal Geographic
Society receptionist whether you can see the view from their sunken
library. While this is a members-only area, my attitude is nothing
ventured, nothing gained.

Opposite: Kynance Mews

STARTING POINT
High Street Kensington
Underground Station

GETTING THERE
District and Circle Lines

Above: Pennant Mews

① MONTPARNASSE CAFÉ
22 Thackeray Street
London W8 5ET
+44 20 7376 2212

② BUILDER'S ARMS
1 Kensington Court Place
London W8 5BJ
+44 20 7937 6213
www.thebuildersarmskensington.co.uk

③ KYNANCE MEWS
Kensington, London SW7 4QR

④ CORNWALL MEWS WEST
Kensington, London SW7 4BH

⑤ PENNANT MEWS
Kensington, London W8 5JN

⑥ THE LITTLE FRENCH RESTAURANT
18 Hogarth Road
London SW5 0QY
+44 20 7370 0366
www.thelittlefrenchrestaurant.com

⑦ AUX MERVEILLEUX DE FRED
88 Old Brompton Road
London SW7 3LQ
+44 20 7584 4249
www.auxmerveilleux.com/home_en

⑧ CINÉ LUMIÈRE
17 Queensberry Place
London SW7 2DT
+44 20 7871 3515
www.institut-francais.org.uk/cine-lumiere

⑨ COMPTOIR LIBANAIS
1–5 Exhibition Road
London SW7 2HE
+44 20 7225 5006
www.comptoirlibanais.com

⑩ NATURAL HISTORY MUSEUM
Cromwell Road
London SW7 5BD
+44 20 7942 2000
www.nhm.ac.uk

⑪ VICTORIA & ALBERT MUSEUM
Cromwell Road
London SW7 2RL
+44 20 7942 2000
www.vam.ac.uk

⑫ SCIENCE MUSEUM
Exhibition Road
London SW7 2DD
+44 870 870 4868
www.sciencemuseum.org.uk

⑬ ROYAL GEOGRAPHICAL SOCIETY
1 Kensington Gore
London SW7 2AR
www.rgs.org

Opposite: Flowers bloom in Kynance Mews

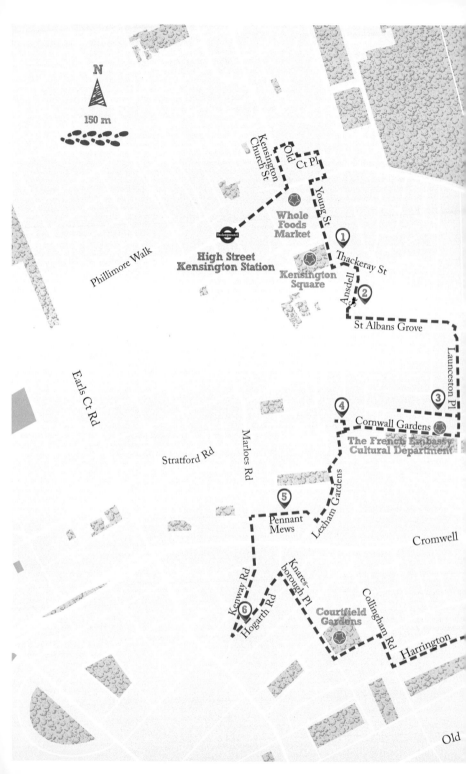

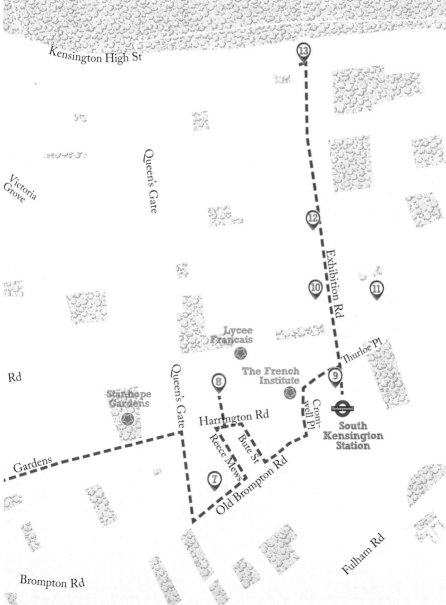

24__ The Dulwich Village Walk
Dulwich to Forest Hill

BEST TIME: Spring; Tuesday through Sunday
DISTANCE: Approximately 5.5 kilometres

With its white picket fences and abundance of greenery, Dulwich has more in common with the Chilterns in rural England than inner-city Brixton 2.5 kilometres away. To demonstrate the parallel universe that you are about to enter, please permit me an anecdote. On the night of the London riots in 2011, a couple of South London friends were scouting for a place to have an early supper. As they wandered through Norwood, SE27, in the late afternoon, all around, shopkeepers and restaurateurs were closing up, pulling down shutters, and scurrying home, hoping to protect their businesses from rioters and looters. More hungry than scared, my friends scratched their heads as to where they could possibly go, and then in unison chorused, "Dulwich!" The pair swears that when they arrived, the streets were strewn with roses whilst sweet violin music serenaded residents dining al fresco. I can well believe the locals feeling impermeable to danger; for Dulwich folk don't look on themselves as real Londoners, hence what happens in the city cannot touch them.

Setting off from West Dulwich BR Station, stroll past the immaculate grounds of ❶ DULWICH COLLEGE, which stretch as far as the eye can see, before turning onto College Road towards the village. The houses along the way are something to behold – discreet mansions set back from the street. It can be fun picking out your favourites, whilst eavesdropping on the elocution of passers-by. Around here, residents don't so much speak the Queen's English as the King's circa 1942; sounding more like they're broadcasting to the nation during the blitz.

Opposite: **Christ's Chapel**

Above: Belair House; Below: Dulwich Village finger signpost

Keeping to the left on College Road, where the picket fence sections off College Gardens, eventually you'll come across a wooden gate that leads down Lovers Walk, which is a delightful rural tract. Continue along and you'll come out the other side, onto Gallery Road. Make a left and you won't have to walk very far before you'll see the entrance gate to Belair Park and, in the foreground of the park, a blanched-white Georgian mansion. This is ❷ BELAIR HOUSE, a Grade II-listed building built in 1785. Beyond the house, you can roam around the artificial lake – originally created by damming the River Effra, which once ran through South London. On completing a loop around the lake, exit the same way you came in and head up Gallery Road.

Soon you'll spot signs for ❸ DULWICH PICTURE GALLERY, a beautiful little exhibition venue set in lovely grounds. Not only is this the oldest public art gallery in England, designed by Regency architect Sir John Soane no less, but it also houses one of the country's finest collections of old continental masters. Poussin, Rubens, Watteau, and Canaletto are all here. Be sure to visit the gallery's mausoleum, which is one of its defining features. Located to the west of the building, it is shaped to recall a funeral monument, with urns atop the building, sarcophagi above the doors, and sacrificial altars in the corners. Inside, the gallery's original five rooms are linked by a series of arches, creating an endless sense of space; with the old and new buildings sympathetically connected by a glass cloister.

Behind the gallery, accessible both from Gallery and College Roads, is the exquisite ❹ CHRIST'S CHAPEL. The best approach is from the gateway where the two roads meet. Pass through the ornamental quadrangle towards the clock tower at the centre of this pristine, Gothic-inspired building, dazzling in the sunlight. The east and west wings were built in the early 1700s and 1800s respectively, whilst the main building dates as far back as the 1600s. You may observe a rustling of curtains from behind the windows of one of the almshouses, which have been turned into modernised flats and let for a modest charge to long-serving parishioners.

Above: Romeo
Jones in Dulwich
Village

The main street is Dulwich Village, where you'll find ⑤ ROMEO JONES, a deli that sells local products like honey produced by Dulwich bees; ⑥ ROCCA DI PAPPA, an excellent Italian restaurant with terraced seating; and a string of boutiques and cafes. Circling back around to Christ's Chapel and the park entrance by way of Turney and Pickwick Roads, you get a sense of local residential life. Access Dulwich Park via College Park entrance, across from the gallery and chapel on College Road.

As you would expect, the village takes great pride in the park's extensive, well-maintained lawns and mature oaks. Head diagonally across the lozenge-shaped park, past the perimeter carriage drive where the trail continues for 100 metres before dividing into lawns. There's a long tradition of boating on the park's lake. The ⑦ PAVILION CAFE, originally named the Refreshment House, was built at the centre of the park in the 1890s. The central footpath beyond leads between the east lawns to the American Garden, occupying a partially sunken area famed for its rhododendrons. Bear right along the trail towards Rosebery Gate, which connects with the South Circular Road.

Take a left and follow South Circular all the way around to ⑧ HORNIMAN MUSEUM AND GARDENS, where you can wander through 16 acres of landscaped parkland. A rather old-school museum, tucked away in Forest Hill, it features exhibits displayed in traditional cases. Look out for the bizarre, overstuffed walrus. There's a quirkily curated permanent gallery dedicated to African, Afro-Caribbean, and Brazilian art; an aquarium; and a collection of approximately 1,600 musical instruments.

Your walk culminates at Forest Hill BR Station, where you can board a train back to the centre of town.

Clockwise from top left: Dulwich Park walking path; Dulwich Park Lodge; Pavilion Café; Rocca di Pappa; Dulwich Park lake; sculpture of Edward Alleyn outside Christ's Chapel

Above: School motto of Dulwich College

STARTING POINT
West Dulwich BR Station

GETTING THERE
Overground from London Victoria

❶ DULWICH COLLEGE
Dulwich Common, London SE21 7LD
+44 20 8693 3601
www.dulwich.org.uk

❷ BELAIR HOUSE
Gallery Road
London SE21 7AB
+44 20 8299 9788
www.belairhouse.co.uk

❸ DULWICH PICTURE GALLERY
Gallery Road
London SE21 7AD
+44 20 8693 5254
www.dulwichpicturegallery.org.uk

❹ CHRIST'S CHAPEL
Gallery Road
London SE21 7
+44 20 8693 1524
www.stbarnabasdulwich.org/
about-us-stb/christ-s-chapel

❺ ROMEO JONES
80 Dulwich Village
London SE21 7BJ
+44 20 8299 1900
www.romeojones.co.uk

❻ ROCCA DI PAPPA
75–79 Dulwich Village
London SE21 7AJ
+44 20 8299 6333
www.roccarestaurants.com/
dulwich_village.htm

❼ PAVILION CAFÉ
Dulwich Park
College Road
London SE21 7BQ
+44 20 8299 1383
www.pavilioncafedulwich.co.uk

❽ HORNIMAN MUSEUM
100 London Road
London SE23 3PQ
+44 20 8699 1872
www.horniman.ac.uk

Opposite: **Dulwich College**

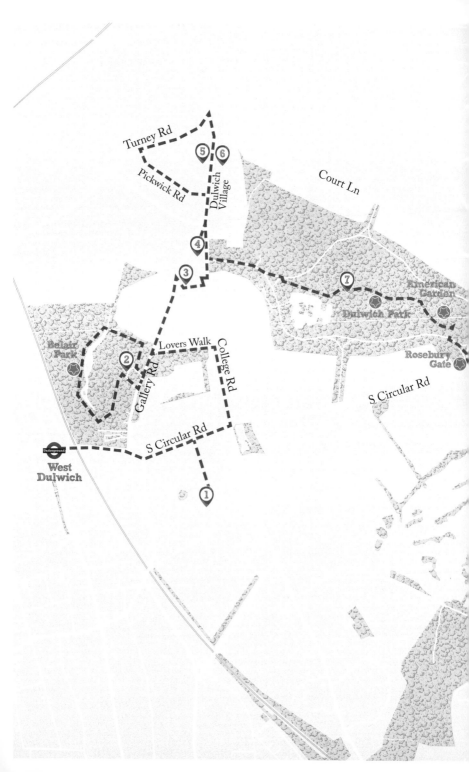

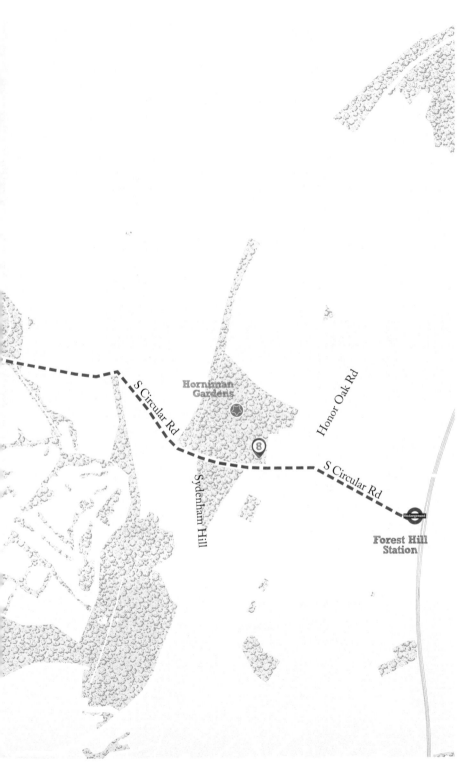

25   The Grand Exhibitors' Walk

Crystal Palace

BEST TIME: Friday, Saturday, or Sunday
DISTANCE: Approximately 5 kilometres

For me, Crystal Palace is akin to linking up with an old childhood friend whom you haven't seen in years – familiar and yet strangely new. Push through the turnstiles at Crystal Palace BR Station, and the cafe ❶ BROWN & GREEN 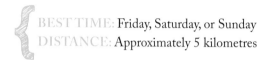, with its lively colours, welcomes you inside. The oversized dimensions of its fixtures – from the exceedingly tall, narrow doors to the forehead-level counter – will leave you feeling like Alice after she's swallowed the shrinking potion.

Exiting the station, bear right into Crystal Palace Park, which was originally landscaped as a Victorian pleasure ground. Across the park you'll see a large tower, which happens to be the fifth tallest structure in London. This is the BBC Transmitter, from where the first colour test transmissions were broadcast to the nation, in 1956. What you won't see is the palace, which was razed to the ground in a fire in 1936. Had Crystal Palace survived, it might have become a national icon akin to the Eiffel Tower; the 20th-century French designer Le Corbusier described it as "one of the great monuments of 19th-century architecture" and declared how he could not tear his eyes "from the spectacle of its triumphant harmony." Made predominantly of glass and cast iron, the structure was enormous, indeed spectacular. Inside, Victorian and Edwardian visitors would have gasped in wonder as they roamed through a series of epic halls, experiencing first-hand the fine art and furnishings of Egyptian, Grecian, and Roman Courts through to medieval and Renaissance times, all lavishly designed. Incredibly, the whole building was prefabricated and assembled at

Opposite: View from Crystal Palace summit

Above: Dinosaur sculptures in Crystal Palace Park; Below: Italian Terraces

Hyde Park for the Great Exhibition in 1851, and then dismantled, shipped, and re-erected on this site in 1854.

Follow the path to your right and you'll soon be face to face with some haughty-looking alpacas, snuffling kune pigs, and fluffy Shetland ponies. Set in a small yard and paddock, ❷ CRYSTAL PALACE PARK FARM is a source of fascination for young and old alike. Be sure that the kids see the reptile room. It'll set them up nicely for what comes next: the Crystal Palace ❸ DINOSAURS.

At first, it may seem absurd to come across 30 crude replicas of prehistoric beasts positioned around a lake fashioned to look like a swamp in the grounds of a suburban park. However unrealistic they may seem now, what's incredible is that these were the first man-made dinosaurs, created only 30 years after dinosaurs were originally discovered. Absurd, certainly, but oddly reflective of Crystal Palace's motivating spirit: to preserve and relish things past.

Stick to the path west of Lower Lake and follow the route past the turnoff to Sydenham Lodge Gate, around the bend, and to the south of Intermediate Lake, where you'll find another piece of faded childhood nostalgia: a ❹ MAZE.

Hidden by a surround of tall trees, the low hedges that make up the maze are not so easy to spot unless you know where to look. Occupying a total area of nearly 2000 square yards, the maze dates back to 1870 and is one of the largest in the country. In its heyday it was a popular place for a stroll after tea, and is still referred to as the "tea maze."

From here, make your way in the direction of the BBC Transmitter and across to the ❺ ITALIAN TERRACES, which are all that survive of the palace. The upper and lower terraces are linked by steps, with sphinxes flanking each flight. It's all rather splendid gazing out over the grounds from here, but imagine how much more impressive this would have been when the original building was encircled by fountains, with thousands of jets of water streaming into the air; and Victorian and Edwardian visitors staring across the night sky at the extravagant displays of fireworks. Traverse the length of the terraces, and you'll come across ⑥ CRYSTAL PALACE MUSEUM. A relatively simple affair, its glass displays and wall illustrations of the Crystal Palace give you a glimpse of the scale of the endeavour and the innovation and imaginativeness of the visionaries involved.

As a child, I would often visit Crystal Palace, never knowing that hidden below the surface of the A212, was a beautifully crafted relic of Victorian construction: the ⑦ CRYSTAL PALACE SUBWAY. Neglected for years and exposed to the elements in places, three sets of grand staircases and the famous brick subway are all that remain of what was once an impressive glass-covered atrium. The organization Friends of Crystal Palace Subway saw the culmination of several years' work when the subway re-opened in 2016. There are regular tours Saturday and Sunday from 10am to 5pm and no pre-booking is required; but the number of people permitted in the subway is limited, so there may be a wait.

Now for an altogether different experience: how about a stroll down to Montmartre? No, you don't have to cross the Channel; only the street. For opposite the bus station, on Crystal Palace Parade, is an attractive-looking bistro with a lively patio area, like something out of a Paris guide.

For years I was both drawn to ⑧ CAFÉ ST GERMAIN and repelled by its location, never venturing inside, much to my loss. It turns out the croque monsieurs and Spanish omelettes, as well as its ambience, are hugely popular with locals.

Pause here for a moment, just a few steps away from the tip of what's known as the Triangle, the hub of Crystal Palace village life, to appreciate another special facet of this place: the views. From the high area around the junction of Westow Hill and Church Road, you can see across to the South Downs or turn towards the city and make out Canary Wharf on a clear day.

A kindred spirit of Stoke Newington in the north, in my reckoning, Crystal Palace has managed to maintain its small-town integrity, staving off forays from coffee and supermarket chains, and championing its many independents. Walking and shopping

Clockwise from top left: Crystal Palace Antiques & Modern store; J. Chittell; Crystal Palace Station sign; Brown & Green Café; The Crystal Palace Market; retro furniture store on Church Road

Above: Haynes Lane Market

the perimeter of the Triangle offers many charming diversions and temptations. Head down Westow Hill, turning off at Jasper Road, and go giddy over the four generous floors of enviable antiques that are spread throughout the gorgeous Victorian warehouse building housing ❾ CRYSTAL PALACE ANTIQUES & MODERN. The shop showcases furniture ranging in design from classic Victorian to Arts & Crafts, Art Deco, and 20th-century Industrial. What makes it all the more fun is that it's so affordable, providing you with the freedom to mentally furnish a dozen rooms in a dozen differently styled homes. Open seven days, 10am to 6pm, the emporium always has new stock coming in, keeping the experience fresh from one week to the next.

Moving on to Westow Street, you'll want to make a right on pretty Haynes Lane. Here you'll find a trove of destinations. Start at ⑩ HAYNES LANE MARKET (open Tuesday, Friday, Saturday, and Sunday, 11am to 5pm), a veritable maze of vintage and vinyl finds crammed into every crevice over two floors. Then on to the weekly Saturday ⑪ FARMERS' MARKET further down the lane, at the intersection with Bedwardine Road. If the ⑫ ART STUDIOS on Haynes Lane happen to be open to the public on the day you are there, you can trot on up the narrow staircase that leads to the warren of painters', photographers', and potters' workspaces for a cup of tea and a chat – and perhaps even invest in the purchase of an original artwork.

Back on Westow Street, you'll pass ⑬ BOOKSELLER CROW ON THE HILL, a vibrant locally owned independent bookshop (an increasingly endangered species in this day and age), followed by a length of road that boasts food for the soul, with Vietnamese restaurant ⑭ URBAN ORIENT and, around the corner on Church Road, another outpost of ⑮ BROWN AND GREEN, well-deservedly popular.

Now for the home stretch. Just when you think you've exhausted a place, Crystal Palace keeps on giving. Having turned onto Church Road, you're spoiled for second-hand retro stores with cheeky-sounding names, like ⑯ FLAMING NORA, which specializes in sourcing upcycled furniture for people wanting something a little different in their homes.

Down-to-earth ⑰ CARTWRIGHT'S deals in antiques, collectibles, and other interesting, quirky rarities, often sourced during house clearances.

Wandering down Annerley Hill, back to the train station, again you are afforded those wonderful views of the outer fringes of urban sprawl and the start of the South Downs. Whatever Crystal Palace is selling, I'm buying.

Crystal Palace BR Station

Overground from London Victoria

**1 BROWN & GREEN
AT THE STATION**
Crystal Palace Station Road
London SE19 2AZ
+44 20 8659 0202
www.brownandgreencafe.com

**2 CRYSTAL PALACE PARK
FARM**
Ledrington Road
London SE19 2BS
+44 20 8659 2557
www.capel.ac.uk/
crystal-palace-park-farm.html

3 DINOSAUR PARK
Crystal Palace Park, London SE19 2GA
+44 300 303 8658
www.cpdinosaurs.org/visitthedinosaurs

4 CRYSTAL PALACE PARK MAZE
Crystal Palace Park
London SE19 2GA

5 ITALIAN TERRACES
Crystal Palace Park, London SE19 2GA

6 CRYSTAL PALACE MUSEUM
Anerley Hill, London SE19 2BA
+44 20 8676 0700
www.crystalpalacemuseum.org.uk

7 CRYSTAL PALACE SUBWAY
Crystal Palace Parade
London SE19 1LG
+44 20 8133 0973
www.cpsubway.org.uk

8 CAFÉ ST GERMAIN
16–17 Crystal Palace Parade
London UK E19 1UD
+44 20 8670 3670
www.cafestgermain.com

**9 CRYSTAL PALACE
ANTIQUES AND MODERN**
Imperial House
Jasper Road
London SE19 1SG
+44 20 8480 7042
www.crystalpalaceantiques.com

**10 HAYNES LANE
MARKET**
Haynes Lane, London SE19 3AN
+44 7968 168532

11 FARMERS' MARKET
Haynes Lane, London SE19 3AP
www.crystalpalacefoodmarket.co.uk

12 OPEN ARTISTS' STUDIOS
Haynes Lane, London SE19
+44 7968 168532

**13 BOOKSELLER CROW
ON THE HILL**
50 Westow Street
London SE19 3AF
+44 20 8771 8831
www.booksellercrow.co.uk

14 URBAN ORIENT
74 Westow Street
London SE19 3AF
+44 20 8616 4511

15 BROWN AND GREEN
99 Church Road
London SE19 2PR
+44 20 8653 3799
www.brownandgreencafe.com

16 FLAMING NORA
40 Church Road
London SE19 2ET
+44 20 7175 0111
www.flaming-nora.com

17 CARTWRIGHT'S
34 Church Road
London SE19 2ET
+44 20 8768 5370
www.cartwrights.london

Opposite: **Crystal Palace Park**

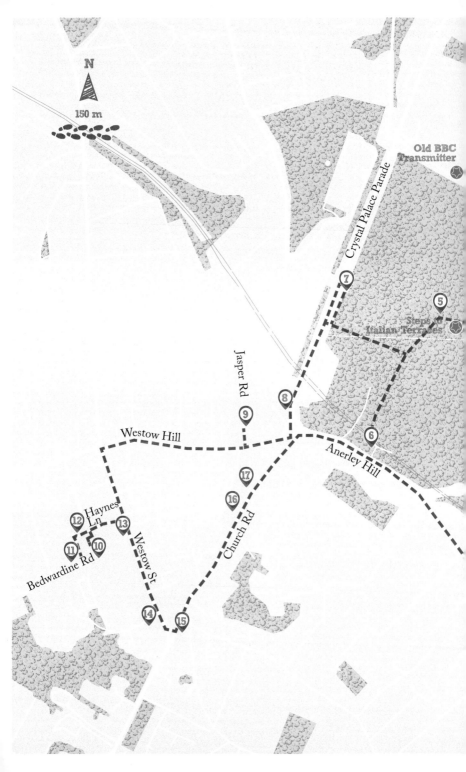

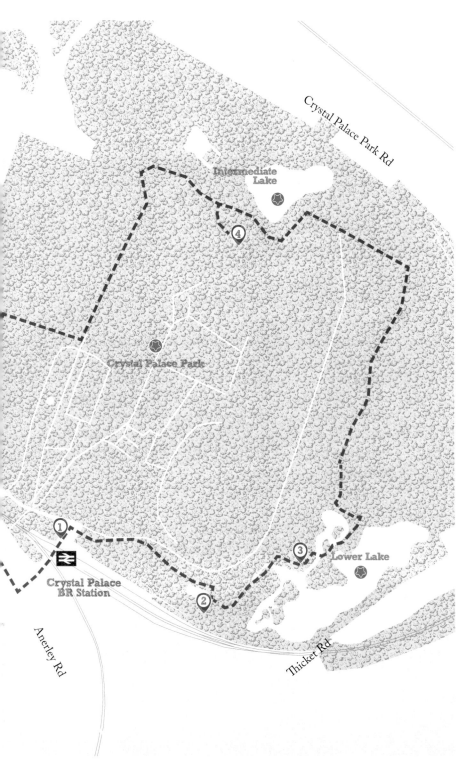

Crystal Palace Park Rd

Intermediate
Lake

④

Crystal Palace Park

①

Crystal Palace
BR Station

Anerley Rd

②

③

Lower Lake

Thicket Rd

26__ The Larders of London Walk

London Bridge to Bermondsey to Tower Bridge

BEST TIME: Saturday morning or afternoon

DISTANCE: Approximately 5 kilometres

So many people *only* come to Borough for the market, but style aficionados know to head here for the hidden enclave of coffeehouses, iconic buildings, and art galleries that dot the area between London and Tower Bridges; whilst those who have ventured further into these backstreets can lay claim to the joyous Maltby Street Market. The whole area hums with life and industry. There's the riverfront promenade, the iconic Borough Market, 19th-century warehouses, the Fashion and Textile Museum, the recently relocated White Cube gallery, and even a spritz of Elizabethan-inspired architecture.

Your walk begins at London Bridge Station. This busy terminus has a surplus of exits, so you'll have to scan for signs for Borough Market. If in doubt, ask someone for directions. Between Borough High Street and ❶ SOUTHWARK CATHEDRAL (which is on a site that has been a place of worship for 1,000 years), ❷ BOROUGH MARKET is nestled beneath a wrought-iron roof by the railway arches, in an area that's been synonymous with food markets since the 11th century. Today, it's where Londoners come in search of prized ingredients for special dinner parties or pricey indulgences. Personally, I come for the ambience: the thrill of hearing the French deli clerk waxing lyrical about which varietal of pimiento olive "madam" should go home with, and the chorus of fishmongers and butchers as they draw the crowds in with their banter.

You'll find the wine bar ❸ BEDALES where Bedale Street intersects with the market under the rail bridges. At this local

Opposite: Borough Market fruit stall

Above: Borough Market; Below: Fish! restaurant, Borough Market

ESTABLISHED 1999

fish!

BOROUGH MARKET

www.fishboroughmarket.com

Restaurant, counter, terrace & take-out

institution in the heart of the market, diners savour the finer things in life, quaffing corked wine accompanied by platters of beautiful patés and cheeses. Come out the far side onto Stoney Street, and you're on the market's more affluent border, where people queue around the block at ❹ MONMOUTH coffee, which has a reputation for roasting the finest coffee beans in town. Another great local watering hole is the ❺ GEORGE INN, tucked in an eponymous yard off Borough High Street. A 17th-century coaching inn and pub with oak beams and a large courtyard seating area, this out-of-the-way place is usually discovered only through an invitation from a friend who lives or works in the area.

Leaving the market for St Thomas Street, weave through the backstreets of Bermondsey. Only a few years ago, one was most likely to take a shortcut down St Thomas for A&E at Guy's Hospital – which is a massive medical complex secreted behind a wall of Victorian terrace buildings. Nowadays, though, the world's rich step out of chauffeur-driven limousines here into the foyer of the five-star Shangri-La Hotel, which occupies nearly 20 floors of Renzo Piano's ultra-modern 95-story glass skyscraper, ❻ THE SHARD. The building's viewing platform, which is open to the public with prior reservation, looks out over the entire capital from a dizzying height.

Old-school Bermondsey was home to the leather making trade for centuries and has an incredible knack for reinvention, absorbing each new change into its constitution seamlessly. Over the years, it has housed 19th-century workhouses; missions; the fur, vinegar, and paper industries; the leather market and tanneries; social housing; and in more recent years, world-class hotels and art galleries.

Turn the corner onto Weston Street, and traditional brick warehouses mix with new residential builds. You may well see a crane hoisting up canvases through a third-floor window, as this area plays host to a thriving artists' community. The stretch of Weston past Snowfields Street gets rather too 1980s for my taste, but I urge you to go on as far as the next turning. This is Ship and Mermaid

Row, more a passageway than a street, which leads you around the ❼ GUINNESS TRUST BUILDINGS, a cluster of beautiful redbrick structures that date back to 1897, which was the year of Queen Victoria's Diamond Jubilee, and now serve as an affordable housing and care complex. The trust was founded by the great-grandson of the Guinness Brewery, Sir Edward Cecil Guinness, for the purpose of providing the city's working poor with decent living quarters.

From here, turn right on Snowfields; cut down Kirby Grove, which borders the Guinness Trust; and wend your way through a section of Leathermarket Gardens back to Weston Street and the historic ❽ LEATHER MARKET. Originally a tannery, the restored yellow-brick Victorian period building is now a co-working space for entrepreneurs and small businesses, and is well worth a view if only from the outside.

From here it's a short stroll to Bermondsey Street via Leathermarket Street, where you'll pass by ❾ THE LEATHER EXCHANGE pub. The building's tannery connection goes as far back as 1879, when this was more a social club than a trading floor, and is memorialised in the roundels depicting scenes from the tanning process. Keep a watchful eye, and you'll find faded signage all around: testament to the area's proud past.

Bermondsey Street is where things really get going, culturally speaking, with the beautifully curated ❿ FASHION AND TEXTILE MUSEUM to your left and ⓫ WHITE CUBE, which is the largest outpost of the well-known contemporary London art gallery, to your right. Then there are the up-and-coming restaurants, fine food stores, and coffeehouses: places like Pizarro and the Watch House.

From here it's several streets over to ⓬ MALTBY STREET MARKET, accessible by way of Tanner or Abbey Street. Nestled under yet more Victorian railway arches, the market is a lively combination of stalls and shops, with additional pop-up bars and eateries happening in the workshops along Ropewalk. This is a less touristy version of Borough Market – earthier and more soulful.

Above: Leathermarket Street sign; Below: Fashion & Textile Museum

Clockwise from top left: Ropewalk; Butler's Wharf; LASSCO Ropewalk; Maltby Street Market; Shad Thames

Wandering through this foodies' nirvana, you won't know where to turn next, as the sweet smell of fresh waffles rises from the hot cast-iron machines at Waffle On and competes with the outdoor coal smoker at African Volcano, where the chefs are cooking up pulled pork. When it comes to chicken soup for the soul, Monty's Deli takes this literally, dishing up soothing, steaming bowls with matzo balls. Ask the guys at the Cheese Truck to grill you a cheese sandwich like your mum used to make. It doesn't stop with food, though;

Above: Steak and Chips stall

there are craft-beer watering holes such as Little Bird Gin and Hiver, selling their Honey Beer. The award for top find, though, goes to ⓭ LASSCO ROPEWALK. LASSCO, short for the London Architectural Salvage and Supply Co, has a longstanding reputation for selling London's best architectural antiques.

Take Tanner Street to Shad Thames, and, as you pass them by, admire the cobblestone streets Queen Elizabeth and Gainsford, with their overhead wrought-iron bridges that take you back to a bygone age. As Shad Thames curves around to the left you'll find yourself along a stretch of shoreline once known as the "Larder of London," dominated by the tea, coffee, spice, and dried fruit warehouses of ⓮ BUTLER'S WHARF. As part of the regeneration of the area, designer and restaurateur Terence Conran opened a number of now well-known riverside restaurants, including ⓯ LE PONT DE LA TOUR, which affords you incredible close-up views of Tower Bridge; particularly special at sunset as daytime fades and the city lights come on.

To end the walk, simply cross over the bridge to Tower Hill Underground Station.

STARTING POINT
London Bridge
Underground Station

GETTING THERE
Northern and/or Jubilee Lines

❶ SOUTHWARK CATHEDRAL
London Bridge, London SE1 9DA
+44 20 7367 6700
www.cathedral.southwark.anglican.org

❷ BOROUGH MARKET
8 Southwark Street
London SE1 1TL
+44 20 7407 1002
www.boroughmarket.org.uk

❸ BEDALES
5 Bedale Street, London SE1 9AL
+44 20 7403 8853
www.bedaleswines.com

❹ MONMOUTH COFFEE
2 Park Street, The Borough
London SE1 9AB
+44 20 7232 3010
www.monmouthcoffee.co.uk

❺ GEORGE INN
The George Inn Yard
75–77 Borough High Street
London SE1 1NH
+44 20 7407 2056
www.george-southwark.co.uk

❻ THE SHARD
32 London Bridge Street
London SE1 9SG
+44 844 499 7111
www.the-shard.com

❼ GUINESS TRUST BUILDINGS
Ship and Mermaid Row, London SE1

❽ THE LEATHER MARKET
Weston Street, London SE1 3ER

❾ THE LEATHER EXCHANGE
15 Leathermarket Street
London SE1 3HN
+44 20 7407 0295
www.leatherexchange.co.uk

❿ FASHION AND TEXTILE MUSUEM
83 Bermondsey Street
London SE1 3XF
+44 20 7407 8664
www.ftmlondon.org

⓫ WHITE CUBE
144–152 Bermondsey Street
London SE1 3TQ
+44 20 7930 5373
www.whitecube.com

⓬ MALTBY STREET MARKET
Ropewalk, London SE1 3PA
+44 7973 705674
www.maltby.st

⓭ LASSCO ROPEWALK
41 Maltby Street, London SE1 3PA
+44 20 7394 8061
www.lassco.co.uk

⓮ LE PONT DE LA TOUR
36D Shad Thames, London SE1 2YE
+44 20 7403 8403
www.lepontdelatour.co.uk

⓯ BUTLER'S WHARF
London SE1 2YD

Opposite: Shad Thames

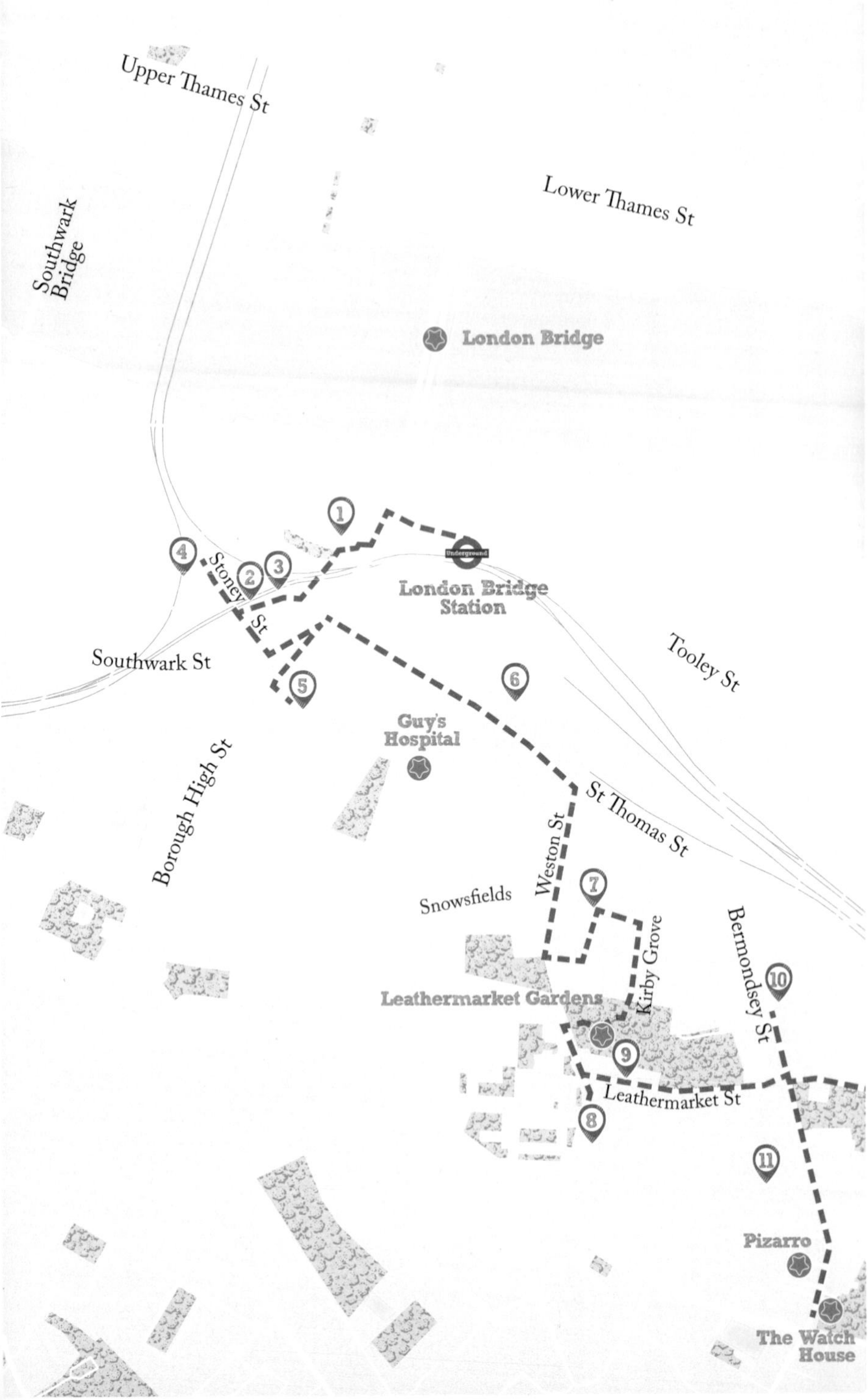

Upper Thames St

Lower Thames St

Southwark Bridge

🛑 London Bridge

④

Stoney St ② ③

① London Bridge Station
Underground

Southwark St

⑤

⑥

Tooley St

Guy's Hospital

Borough High St

St Thomas St

Weston St

Snowsfields

⑦

Kirby Grove

Leathermarket Gardens

Bermondsey St

⑩

⑨

Leathermarket St

⑧

⑪

Pizarro

The Watch House

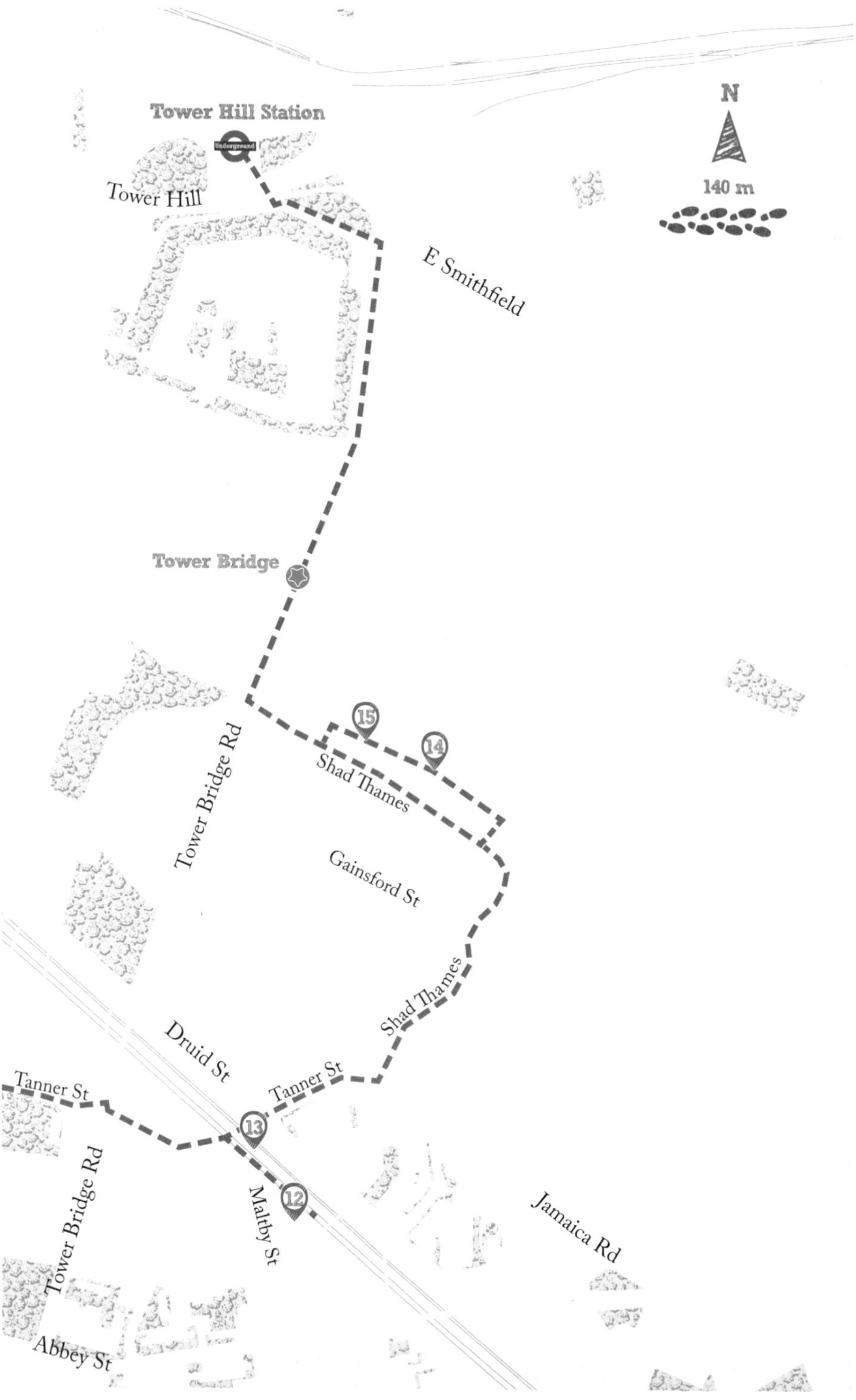

N

140 m

Tower Hill Station

Underground

Tower Hill

E Smithfield

Tower Bridge

Tower Bridge Rd

(15)

(14)

Shad Thames

Gainsford St

Shad Thames

Druid St

Tanner St

Tanner St

Tanner St

(13)

(12)

Maltby St

Jamaica Rd

Tower Bridge Rd

Abbey St

WEST
LONDON ♥

27 __ The Treasure Hunt Walk

Notting Hill to Portobello Road

BEST TIME: Saturday, for Portobello Market
DISTANCE: Approximately 5 kilometres

Notting Hill is best known for its annual carnival and its weekly market. Every August, for the past 50 years, the West Indian community has hosted one of the world's largest street festivals, attracting millions, and every Saturday, for almost 70 years, thousands of dealers have transformed Portobello Road into a major antiques fair. With all its treasures, Portobello Road has always been a place for people aspiring to the "better life," or those craving the riches of the past – but first you'll have to find it.

It can prove elusive for first-timers. For ease and efficiency, setting off from Ladbroke Grove is a safe bet, but for those looking to mine more than merchandise, Notting Hill Gate is the place to begin your treasure hunt. Exiting the station, turn down Pembridge Road and you'll pass the ❶ GATE THEATRE, the smallest "off-West End" theatre in London. Just after the roundabout is a small parade of fashion and vintage shops. The pizza place (Arancina), with the orange Cinquecento car in the window front, is rather popular. The first turning on your left is the start of *the* street, Portobello Road, with its iconic signpost lettering and shop façades in a colourful array of pastel shades. But let us take the scenic route today instead, and loop around to the main event; for good things come to those who wait.

Heading down Chepstow Crescent to Ledbury Road, admire the gracious proportions of the houses on the streets surrounding Portobello. Before long you'll come to ❷ BEACH BLANKET BABYLON, an opulent club for London's playboys situated in a Georgian mansion. It's worth stopping to have a mosey around

Opposite: Portobello Road

its decadent interior. Reaching Westbourne Grove, you've arrived at one of the most privileged pockets of Notting Hill. With its Joseph boutique, artisanal brasserie/designer furniture fusion shop (Daylesford), and al fresco dining, this street is a playground for W11's elite. Even the Oxfam charity shop boasts designer wear, and matching high prices. But gentrification is only one side to this multifaceted neighbourhood.

Venture on along Ledbury, salivating over the opulent-looking macaroons and meringues in Ottolenghi's shop window, before turning onto Talbot Road. Along the way, you'll pass a true Portobello stronghold, a bastion for the arts, ❸ THE TABERNACLE. Peer through the wrought-iron gates to the large courtyard area fronting the curved Romanesque façade of the redbrick and terra-cotta building beyond. Back in the 1950s, this area was the focal point for the race riots, with fascists and Teddy boys descending, and locals (a vibrant Caribbean community) responding to the violence and negativity by establishing the Notting Hill Carnival. Both Muhammad Ali and Malcolm X made pilgrimages to perform at the Tabernacle, and the neighbourhood has always fought for its survival, in 1973 even going so far as to lock councillors in at a meeting at All Saints Hall – around the corner on Powis Gardens – to force them to listen to their demands, which included opening the Tabernacle as a community centre.

It's hard to believe that 50 years ago, this was a no-go area, whereas, these days, Notting Hill is one of the most expensive and hip parts of London, rebranded "Noho" by the aspirational set (a nod to London's trendy Soho).

Leaving the Tabernacle behind, you'll spy the hoi polloi drifting along in the distance. That's because you're no more than a few blocks from the main attraction, Portobello Market. But I'd like to tease you with the promise of Portobello for a while longer and share a few more of its offshoots before the grand finale.

Opposite: Pembridge Road

Carry on down Talbot Road and, at All Saints Church, make a right onto Clydesdale followed by a right onto Westbourne Park Road and a quick left onto All Saints Road. Off the beaten track, this street may be a fraction of the length of Portobello, but it's certainly on the map with locals. For decades, London cyclists knew to head here for the Bicycle Workshop (now sadly closed down), whilst musicians come from far and wide to shop for instruments at Portobello Music. Anyone looking for an evening meal would do well to reserve a table at the Ripe Tomato.

At the end of the street, turn right onto Tavistock Crescent and then follow the bend of the road around to the left and cross over the train tracks via the pedestrian bridge. On the other side, bear right on Acklam Road and right again onto St Ervans Road. When you reach Golborne Road, you'll have gone farther than most visitors. This crucial artery off Portobello is sometimes known as Little Morocco, due to the number of Moroccan restaurants and shops, and is also renowned in the Portuguese community for the two Portuguese pâtisseries, Café O'Porto and Lisboa. Every day except Sunday, Golborne Road hosts a street market specialising in produce, with hot food and knickknacks at the weekend. It has the reputation for being like Portobello was 20 years ago: plenty of real junk, but also the place to pick up on new trends.

Truly, though, you'll only get a sense of a neighbourhood when you've sat down in the one dyed-in-the wool establishment any local worth their salt frequents. At the bottom of Golborne, that place is the ❹ GOLBORNE DELI. Take a pew inside, and let the accents of London traders and creative media types, old Caribbean gentlemen, Middle-Eastern merchants, and French, German, Italian, and Spanish visitors and students conversing in their own languages wash over you. Check out the eclectic crowd, for there is a magnetic quality to Notting Hill that attracts true characters – not just "types" but genuine people who have an I-have-suffered, lived-life, been-around-the-world, seen-all-manner-of-things, can-laugh-at-it-all quality to them. From the deli, turn left onto

Clockwise from top left: Portobello Road; local bookshop; Pembridge Road; The Portobello Kitchen; town houses on Portobello Road; Antique Arcade

Above: Portobello Road street sign; Below: Pembridge Road

the bottom of Portobello, where the bric-a-brac end of the market is located.

300 metres along, you'll come to the Westway (that'll be the concrete flyover rising above the street). For those who welcome scouting around for fashion buys, this is the place to head. Here you'll find the stalls of second-hand clothes dealers side-by-side with those of young designers who are trying to get their wares out there. Passing beneath the Westway, you can browse collectibles of all kinds, from vinyl to posters to military memorabilia. Come August and the Notting Hill Carnival, this entire stretch is cleared to make room for 20 miles of colourful costumes and hundreds of thousands of revellers. Not the best day for a walk – but well worth experiencing.

Next come the fruit and veg stands, followed by flowers and even more goodies. Advance and you could be tricked into believing that you're on a film set or in an MTV music video shoot. For, while East London has elements of a made-for-radio play, West London moves more like a catwalk. Hugh Jackman has been seen strolling along Portobello and, of course, you may recognize many of the locations featured in the 1999 romcom *Notting Hill*, with Julia Roberts and Hugh Grant, which was filmed here.

Around Blenheim Crescent, you might experience the urge to "peek behind the curtain" at what lies in the surrounding streets. Kensington Park Road is where shoppers go to step out of the fray and unwind over a coffee or something stronger. Between Elgin Crescent and Blenheim Crescent, you can still hear the sounds of the market and buskers playing the sax or guitar. Here, you'll also find a readers' paradise, ❺ LUTYENS & RUBINSTEIN, a literary agency-cum-bookshop. If you follow the spiral staircase to the basement, don't be surprised if you see the shelves slide open to reveal the secret room behind. That's where the agents hide out.

Surely, you must be hungry by now, what with the smell of street food cooking and the sight of locals scurrying home laden with

Above: Pembridge Road

grocery bags. On Portobello, there are bakeries and delis aplenty for those after an artisanal backdrop, or the Electric Diner for something more upmarket. Or you can simply grab a bite from one of the stalls and keep moving. Wash it all down, though, with the best cup of coffee in town, at another local stalwart, the Coffee Plant, opposite the popular ❻ ELECTRIC CINEMA, which claims to be the oldest working movie theatre in the UK.

Nearing the final stretch, you'll find the antiques dealers holding court along the four blocks from Colville Terrace to Chepstow Villas. As the song goes, "Dented and tarnished, scarred and unvarnished. In old Portobello they're bought and they're sold." The antiques arcades are a unique feature of Portobello. The entrances are often obscured by booths in front, but do persevere, as beyond these are labyrinths full of stalls offering a host of different types of antiques. The ❼ ADMIRAL VERNON ANTIQUES MARKET, spread over two storeys, is the largest arcade at Portobello Road. With more than 200 dealers, it is the place to find a wide range of items, including curiosities, jewellery, silverware, glass, old clocks, toys, military items and guns, books, paintings, and decorative objects.

I so hope that, by the time you return to Pembridge Road and Notting Hill Gate, you'll have encountered some of the people who make this neighbourhood so memorable: the stallholders and musicians, the restaurateurs and shopkeepers, the longstanding locals and residents who have settled here for the duration.

Above: Electric Cinema; Below: Admiral Vernon Antiques

Above: Portobello Road

STARTING POINT
Notting Hill Gate
Underground Station

GETTING THERE
Hammersmith &
City or Circle Lines

❶ GATE THEATRE
11 Pembridge Road, London W11 3HQ
+44 20 7229 0706
www.gatetheatre.co.uk

❷ BEACH BLANKET BABYLON
45 Ledbury Road, London W11 2AA
+44 20 7229 2907
www.beachblanket.co.uk

❸ THE TABERNACLE
34–35 Powis Square, London W11 2AY
+44 20 7221 9700
www.tabernaclew11.com

❹ GOLBORNE DELI
100 Golborne Road,
London W10 5PS
+44 20 8969 6907
www.golbornedeli.com

❺ LUTYENS &
RUBENSTEIN
21 Kensington Park Road
London W11 2EU
+44 20 7229 1010
www.lutyensrubinstein.co.uk

❻ ELECTRIC CINEMA
191 Portobello Road
London W11 2ED
+44 20 7908 9696
www.electriccinema.co.uk

❼ ADMIRAL VERNON
ANTIQUES MARKET
141–149 Portobello Road
London W11 2DY
+44 20 7727 5242

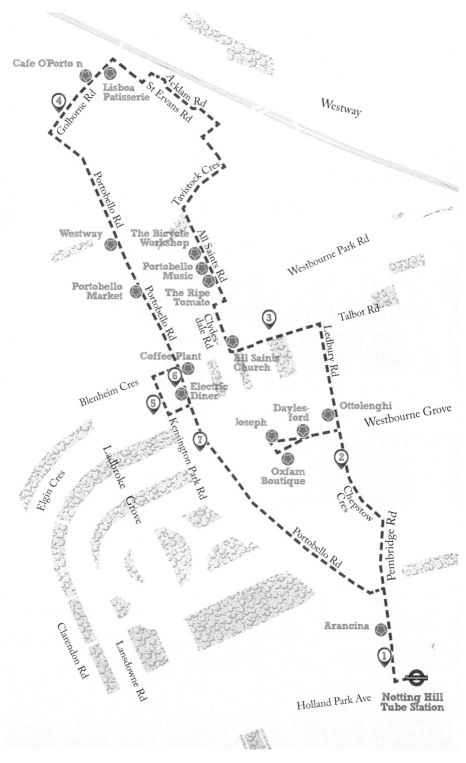

28__ The Art Lovers' Walk

Ladbroke Grove to Holland Park

BEST TIME: Spring; Wednesday, Saturday, or Sunday afternoon

DISTANCE: Approximately 5 kilometres

Wending your way from Ladbroke Grove towards Holland Park, you'll be led into a land of peacocks, Orientalism, and Victoriana. This walk promises all these curiosities and more. Given the quality of light reflected off the alabaster-hued, terraced Victorian houses, it should also come as no surprise to hear how many artists and art lovers have called this neighbourhood home.

Setting off from the Ladbroke Grove tube station, head uphill along Ladbroke Grove, away from the railway bridge. At the fifth turning on your right, follow the curve of Elgin Crescent around, admiring the grand sweep of the impeccably presented residences as you do. This is the jewel in the crown of the Ladbroke Estate, with its grand stucco frontages and its large private communal gardens (accessible only if you are in possession of a key), originally known as "pleasure grounds" or "paddocks," enclosed by terraces and/or crescents of houses. Back in 1837, the Hippodrome racecourse ran around this hill, and spectators were expected to watch from the summit. Heading in the direction of Avondale Park, by way of Portland Road, you'll spot an architectural oddity set into a decidedly 1970s-looking residential estate on Walmer Road. This is the renovated 19th-century ❶ BOTTLE KILN, a throwback to less-salubrious times, when the local industry was pig farming. Certainly, this is a far cry from the tone of the neighbourhood today.

Complete a loop back around to Clarendon Road by way of Hippodrome Place into Clarendon Cross, and along the way you'll come across one of the area's best-kept secrets: ❷ JULIE'S. I still remember the first time I walked through this restaurant's doors. French jazz music was wafting from the speakers in the champagne

Opposite: Frescoes, Holland Park cloisters

Above: Holland Park neighbourhood; Below: Elgin Crescent

bar, and our waiter, who was delighted to hear this was our inaugural visit, invited us on a tour of the building. Nothing can prepare you for the labyrinthine quality of the rooms in back, from the stately Provençal room at street level to the cellar area, with its intimate candlelit alcoves and medieval banquet hall. Back upstairs, there's the low-ceilinged mezzanine with even lower tables, cushioned seating, and tables set for a Middle-Eastern feast. Descend a white wrought-iron spiral staircase beyond, and you're in the light-filled garden room, which is rumoured to have its own haunted resident: the lady in white, who likes to dine on Sundays.

Here, I would draw your gaze to the route marked out on the map (p. 319). I came to so enjoy meandering up and down these streets, postponing the pleasure of Holland Park's roses, Japanese-inspired garden, and woodland; for this residential enclave claims many charms of its own. Enter this maze of streets from Lansdowne Rise, taking in ❸ ST JOHN'S CHURCH, which was built as the original centrepiece of the Ladbroke Estate. Characterized by terraces of stuccoed brick houses backing onto large private garden squares, the area features many original Victorian buildings – as can be seen by walking a full turn around Stanley and Lansdowne Crescents. If you're fortunate enough to be here in June, during Open Square Gardens, you'll have the rare privilege of wandering through some of the more private properties. At this annual event, generous London residents throw open their gardens to visitors over the course of a week-end. A genteel party spirit prevails, so long as the weather does too.

There is one last landmark to take in before reaching the park. See that lofty Art Nouveau mansion block situated on the eastern side of Lansdowne Road? Scottish architect William Flockhart designed the eight-storey tower of apartments and studios for South-African mining magnate Sir Edmund Davis in 1904 to accommodate artist Charles Shannon and his devoted artist friend Charles Ricketts. Since then, ❹ LANSDOWNE HOUSE has undergone a number of alterations and now consists of 13 self-contained flats. From the street, though, what draws your eye is the large multi-paned windows, promising vaulted ceilings and the prospect of incredible natural light inside. There are also multiple blue plaques to commemorate former residents, most of them distinguished artists, as Ladbroke had something of a reputation as an artistic quarter.

And so, at last, you'll find yourself one street away from Holland Park. Returning to the map, you'll see that there are multiple entry points to the park – yet none can top the delightful feeling of walking into the secret garden through the arched wooden gate set into the long Jacobean wall that traverses Holland Park Avenue.

Of all London's parks, this is the most romantic and serene. Wandering up the steep incline into the wooded section, stroll down the second path on your right until you reach the Lord Holland Memorial, and the intersection where the path diverges in five directions. Circling the memorial clockwise, take the third path on your left. After about 100 metres, turn left and then left again into the ❺ KYOTO GARDEN. Exit at the far south of the gardens and, where the path intersects with a second path, keep going straight and you will pass the peacock enclosure. From here, bear right and head toward the Belvedere restaurant. Turn left just before the restaurant and loop around the formal rose gardens to ❻ THE ORANGERY's courtyard, which adjoins the Belvedere. On warm days, friends sit picnicking on blankets around the fountain. Admire the fresco paintings along the cloisters before wandering east, past the park's cafe, towards Holland House, which forms a backdrop for the open-air theatre that is home to ❼ OPERA HOLLAND PARK. Evening performances are splendid affairs, with ladies dressed to the nines and gentlemen in dinner jackets – like something out of *Brideshead Revisited*. Not even many locals get to experience this side of London life. Retrace your steps to the cafe and follow the path around to the left, keeping parallel to the playing fields.

Next, you'll want to take the south-west park exit down Ilchester Place, which merges into Melbury Road. Turn right on Holland Park Road and you are now in the Royal Borough of Kensington and Chelsea. In the mid-19th century, a unique colony of artists'

Clockwise from top left: Holland Park –
entrance on Holland Park Avenue; frescoes
in the park's cloisters; the rose gardens;
The Belvedere restaurant; The Orangery;
fresco detail

residences grew up around ❽ LEIGHTON HOUSE, the home of Lord Frederick Leighton, now a museum that's open to the public. Known as the Holland Park Circle, these individuals became the backbone of the artistic establishment, enjoying great wealth and fame. Lord Leighton and George Frederic Watts, two artists at the heart of the group, were close friends who often called on each other through a gate that connected their gardens. Allow yourself to be drawn into the museum's shaded interior, to marvel at the Arab Hall, its walls lined with beautiful Islamic tiles. The small, tranquil pool sunken in the floor affords a moment of quiet reflection. Moving through the interconnected rooms on the ground level, savour the original Victorian and Orientalist artwork. Upstairs, Leighton's vast studio was one of the sights of London, filled with his paintings in various stages of completion, lit by a great north window. Many of the most prominent figures of the Victorian age were entertained in this room; including Queen Victoria herself, who called on Leighton in 1859. Music lovers still come here to enjoy classical recitals in the evenings.

The history and design buffs among you will particularly appreciate the next stop. Return to Melbury Road, heading south, and then make your way east along Kensington High Street. Turn left on Phillmore Gardens, and then turn right on Stafford Terrace. ❾ NO. 18 is the former residence of *Punch* cartoonist Edward Linley Sambourne, his wife, Marion, their two children, and their live-in servants. The home provides a rare example of the "House Beautiful" style. This can be seen throughout the well-preserved interior, which includes various original Japanese, Middle-Eastern, and Chinese objects. In 1980, the property was opened to the public by the Victorian Society.

As you near the end of your walk, there are several options open to you. You can hop on the tube at High Street Kensington, complete your circuit by returning to Notting Hill, or – for those of you with sturdier calves and a hardier constitution – carry on to Museum Mile and the *French Quarter Walk* (p. 252).

Opposite: Lord Holland Statue

317

Above: Holland Park streets

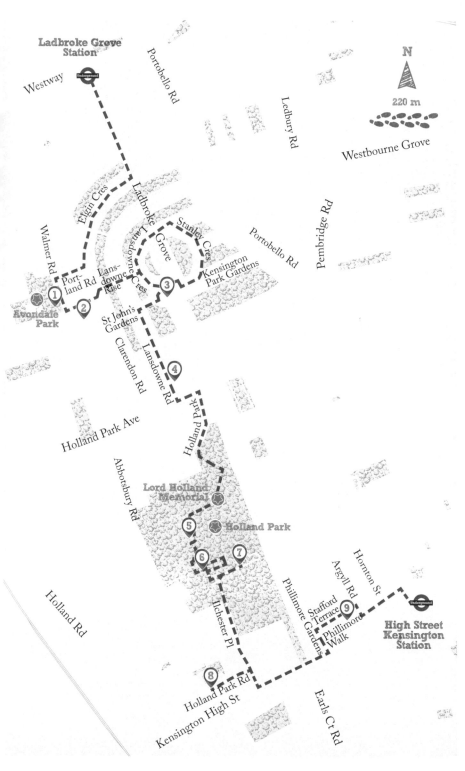

29 The Arcadian Walk

Little Venice to St John's Wood to Regent's Park

BEST TIME: Spring or summer
DISTANCE: Approximately 8 kilometres

Upon first hearing of a place in London called Little Venice, my imagination ran wild. Would there be Italian gondoliers, a piazza, and a skyline of domed buildings? Whilst the reality is hardly Venetian (replace gondolas and palatial homes crumbling into seawater with waterbuses and houses set back on leafy avenues), the area does have some sympathy with its namesake, for example an air of rare seclusion, an appreciation for beauty, and of course its canal.

Stepping out of Warwick Avenue Station, you are betwixt Lisson Grove and St John's Wood, both fashionable areas of the Regency period, owned and developed by the Eyre Estate. Many of the leases and the land are still owned by Eyre descendants and this broad street – with its white, stuccoed villas – is typical of the period. The distinctive cream-colored façades line both sides of the canal and, in the early 1800s, they would have attracted the literary and journalistic set, George Eliot among them.

While you are welcome to walk Warwick Avenue to the canal, I suggest delaying and instead circling around to Clifton Villas by way of Warrington Crescent and Formosa Street, so as to end up at Bristol Gardens. While these are mere mid-sized Regency terraced houses, the street is gratifyingly dignified.

Ahead of you, there is a small, open passageway, which leads through to ❶ CLIFTON NURSERIES, part garden centre and part sanctuary for savvy locals in search of a secret hideaway. The passageway opens up into a charming courtyard, a secluded spot in which to sit outside on warmer days, with an attractive indoor greenhouse cafe for wetter ones.

Opposite: **Little Venice Canal**

Above: Café LaVille; Below: Example of a mid-terrace house on Hamilton Close

At the end of the Clifton Villas, before turning left onto Blomfield Road, you'll see ❷ THE SUMMERHOUSE seafood restaurant just to your right, which has a terrace overlooking the canal. The nearest bridge is Westbourne Terrace Road, a popular spot for boarding a boat for a canal ride.

Walk the length of canal-facing Blomfield Road, and the neighbourhood feels more townlike, reflective of the streets a Jane Austen character might have strolled two centuries ago in Bath or Cheltenham. If your knowledge of English architectural periods is as hazy as mine, then it might interest you to know that the principal difference between Regency houses and their late Georgian equivalents is their size. The taller Regency fronts – with their use of stucco, heavy cornices, and decorative ironwork – continued to be classical in style, but they lost the neat proportions of their Georgian predecessors. Another significant difference was the half basement of the Regency house, which raised the ground floor by several steps above street level.

At the busy intersection of Blomfield and Edgeware Roads, look out for ❸ CAFE LAVILLE, straddling the canal. Step inside, and you'll be treated to one of the finest cafe views in all of London: a huge landscape window through which to gaze the length of the canal.

From here, wend your way along Aberdeen Place and Cunningham Place to St John's Wood Road and ❹ HAMILTON CLOSE, a mews which would once have been the stables for a local aristocratic household, and then to Hamilton Terrace, another fine example of a leafy Regency-style broad street.

Back in the 1800s, men of certain means could buy a great deal of privacy here, in what was then considered the outer realms of mainstream London society. Far behind these high walls, a gentleman could ensconce his mistress or welcome a lover. The rumour goes that there have been kept women in parts of St John's Wood as far back as the Restoration. Others took advantage of the villas' privacy, installing several "laundresses" (a term coined for a house of ill repute) and even lunatic asylums, where wealthy patrons could deposit sons and daughters, wives and siblings. Regularly, Lord Eyre would receive news of such goings-on. A rather open-minded man for the times, he would write to the transgressor merely advising them to marshal their private affairs so as to not spill out onto the streets. When a "homosexual" scandal arose, with residents notifying his lordship of one tenant's known associations with convicted "deviants," the earl, admirably, went against the grain and refused to evict said gentleman.

Where Hamilton Terrace meets Hall Road, steer to the right. The tone of your walk will change somewhat at the next turning — a left on Grove End. After 100 yards or so, you'll spot a most incongruous sight: groups of tourists assembling in packs of four, halting traffic as they march along a pedestrian crossing, arms swinging in unison. For this is the start of ❺ ABBEY ROAD (the nearby ❻ ABBEY ROAD STUDIOS is where the Beatles recorded their famous album) and what you are witnessing is a re-enactment of the iconic *Abbey Road* album cover.

Retracing your steps along Grove End Road in the direction of the canal, make a left turn on St John's Wood Road, but not before noting Lisson Grove across the street. In the 1800s, this area was a magnet for theatre people as well as musicians, artists, architects, and writers. A coterie of painters from the Royal Academy settled here, congregating around William Blake.

Continuing along St John's Wood Road, you'll pass the famous ❼ LORD'S CRICKET GROUND on your left. Lord's opened here in 1814, around the same time as John Nash, director of the Regent's Canal Company, began building detached villas set in gardens facing the canal. Nash was also the architect of our final destination: Regent's Park.

At the roundabout up ahead, come off at St John's Wood Church and wander through the gardens to St John's Wood High Street, which is worth a gander, especially if you're in need of watering or

Opposite: Abbey Road

324

All pictures: Sights and scenes in Regent's Park.

the use of some facilities, but then it's on to Regent's Park by way of Prince Albert Road.

Entering the park at Avenue Road, cross over the canal to the Outer Circle, which runs the park's circumference. Here on the north-western edge are the principal six ❽ DETACHED VILLAS designed by the English neoclassical architect Quinlan Terry. Terry designed each house in a different classical style. To observe the mix of Corinthian and Tuscan villas interspersed amongst the predominant Regency architecture, make a right onto Outer Circle, and loop around at the second turning on your left, getting up close to Winfield House, the official residence of the US ambassador.

Returning to the path you entered the park on, continue straight ahead until you reach a fork in the walkway. Stay to the right, and at the next fork, keep to the western flank of the park and follow the curve of the Boating Lake to a bridge. Cross over and continue on the path until you arrive at Inner Circle.

When John Nash was designing the 395-acre park, this central ring was to have been the spot reserved for the Prince Regent's Palace. Today, as well as being the most carefully tended section of the park, it boasts a theatre and the Regent's Cafe. The wall to your left surrounds the ❾ OPEN AIR THEATRE, where wonderful productions of Shakespeare's plays are put on throughout the summer to delight audiences. Originally, the ornamental gardens here were landscaped by the Royal Botanic Society. When the society's lease expired, in 1932, ❿ QUEEN MARY'S GARDENS were born, culminating in a cascade, rose gardens (containing more than 400 varieties of roses), and the small ⓫ JAPANESE GARDEN ISLAND.

Crossing Inner Circle again, follow the signs for York Bridge. The large buildings on your right are Regents University London and the European Business School. York Bridge will lead you over the tail end of the Boating Lake and left onto Ulster Terrace on the south side of Outer Circle. The wonderfully named architect Decimus Burton fulfilled Nash's vision for the grand terraced housing you see here. Make a right on Park Square West and walk up to the busy main road. Turn left here onto Marylebone Road and cross over at the set of traffic lights for Park Crescent, which forms a semi-circle around a private garden.

Not many people know that there is an underpass linking the private gardens of Park Crescent to the private gardens of Park Square on the other side of Marylebone Road. This was known as Nursemaids' Tunnel and is still in use today. The public rarely has access to it, however, except during the annual Open Garden Squares weekend in June.

Here our Regency Walk draws to an end at the steps leading down from Marlyebone Road to Regent's Park Underground Station.

STARTING POINT
Warwick Avenue Underground Station
GETTING THERE
Bakerloo Line

1 CLIFTON NURSERIES
5A Clifton Villas
London W9 2PH
+44 20 7289 6851
www.clifton.co.uk

2 THE SUMMERHOUSE
60 Blomfield Road
London W9 2PA
+44 20 7286 6752
www.thesummerhouse.co

3 CAFÉ LAVILLE
453 Edgware Road
London W2 1HT
+44 20 7706 2620

4 HAMILTON CLOSE
London NW8 8QY

5 BEATLES' ABBEY ROAD CROSSING
2 Abbey Road, London NW8 0AH

6 ABBEY ROAD STUDIOS
3 Abbey Road, London NW8 9AY
+44 20 7266 7000
www.abbeyroad.com

7 LORD'S CRICKET GROUND
St John's Wood Road
London NW8 8QN
+44 20 7616 8500
www.lords.org

8 QUINLAN TERRY'S REGENT'S PARK VILLAS
Regent's Park, London NW1 4HB

9 OPEN AIR THEATRE
Regent's Park
London NW1 4NU
+44 844 826 4242
www.openairtheatre.org

10 QUEEN MARY'S GARDENS
Chester Road, London NW1 4NR

11 JAPANESE GARDEN ISLAND
Regent's Park, London NW1 4NR
www.sequinsandcherryblossom.com

Opposite: **Regent's Park**

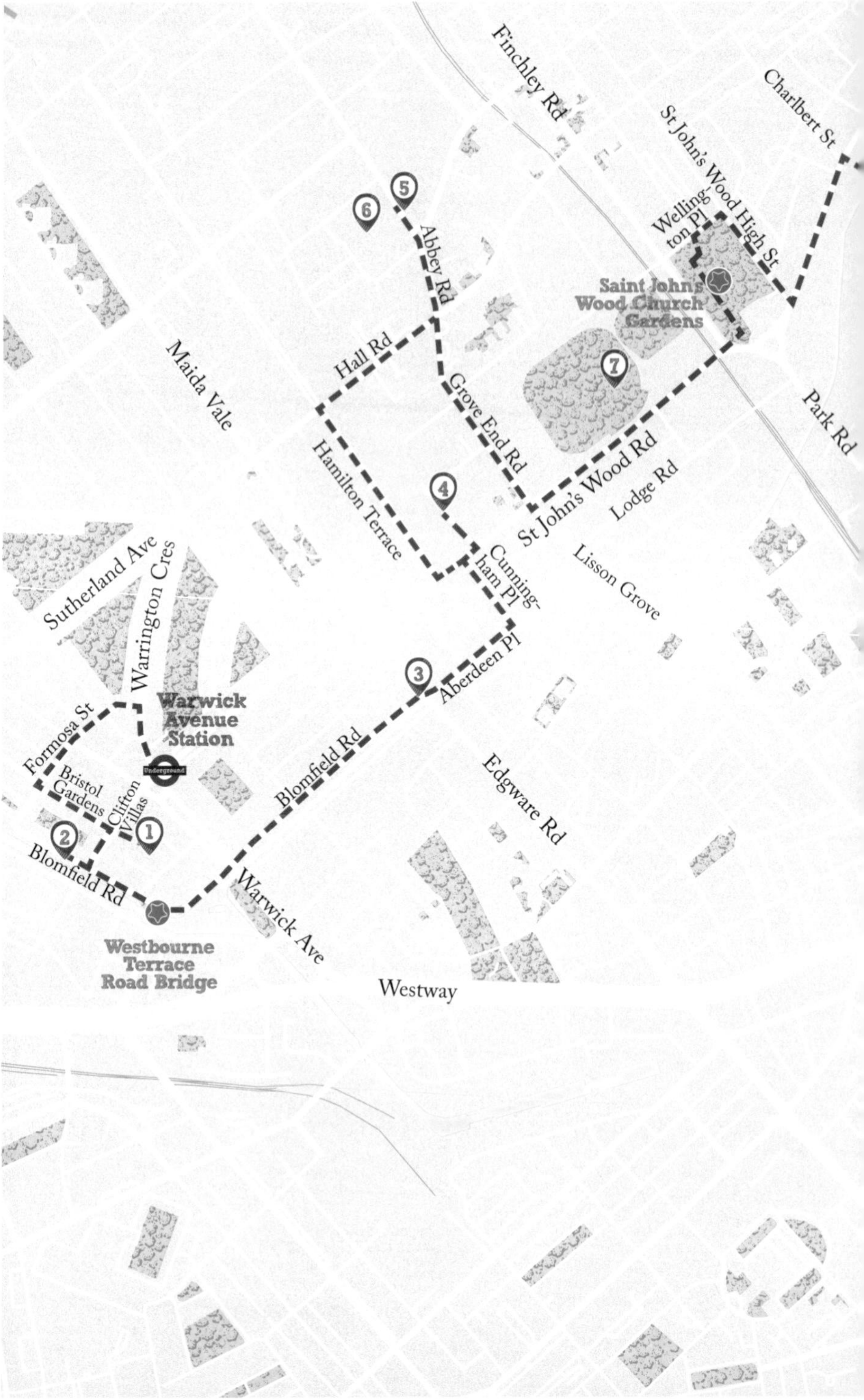
Finchley Rd
Charlbert St
St John's Wood High St
Welling-
ton Pl
Saint John's
Wood Church
Gardens
Abbey Rd
Hall Rd
Maida Vale
Grove End Rd
Park Rd
Hamilton Terrace
St John's Wood Rd
Lodge Rd
Lisson Grove
Cunning-
ham Pl
Sutherland Ave
Warrington Cres
Aberdeen Pl
Warwick
Avenue
Station
Formosa St
Underground
Blomfield Rd
Edgware Rd
Bristol
Gardens
Clifton
Villas
Blomfield Rd
Warwick Ave
Westbourne
Terrace
Road Bridge
Westway
1
2
3
4
5
6
7

30__ The River Walk

Putney to Hammersmith

BEST TIME: Summer
DISTANCE: Approximately 4 kilometres

Come the last weekend in March/first weekend in April, middle England – and a fair few Antipodeans – descends on Putney for the annual Cambridge vs. Oxford University boat race. People have been flocking to this long-running national event for more than a century and a half to cheer on these men (and now women) in blue – with Cambridge in light blue and Oxford in dark blue – as they race each other from Putney to Mortlake, 4 miles downriver. Up to 250,000 spectators gather each year for an event that is over in less than 20 minutes. They don straw boater hats and blazers (often old public-school ones, recovered from Ma and Pa's place in the country), and arrive carrying pitchers of Pimms from some nearby waterfront bar. Covertly, it's become more of an excuse for the first outdoors knees-up of the year, so best for walkers to avoid the area that particular weekend.

Moving down Station Approach from Putney Bridge Underground, continue on to Gonville Street and across the A219 at the traffic lights, to All Saints Church opposite. Hidden in back is ❶ FULHAM PALACE GARDENS, which is fitting given that this historic site has had close links to the church for over 1300 years and been home to successive bishops of London. Its medieval past can still be seen in vestiges of the moat that once encircled the palace. Because of its adjacency to a vital Thames crossing, the Romans would have had a settlement here too. From the gardens, you can enter the palace grounds, free of charge.

Bear right, wandering through the 13 acres of lawn and gardens. Long before you reach the palace, you'll encounter the 18th-century

Opposite: **Riverside Walk sign**

◄ ᴛʜᴀᴍᴇꜱ ᴘᴀᴛʜ

RIVERSIDE
WALK  ►

Clockwise from top left: **Bishops Park; Fulham Palace; Walled Garden; Fulham Palace grounds and Bishops Park**

❷ WALLED GARDEN, which has wisteria running along its sides. Behind those walls, the garden paths are laid out traditionally, with abundant ornamental planting all around. Look out for some stunning dahlias. You can wander between the knot garden, with its colourful perennial display of red, blue, and yellow irises and roses – in bloom during the summer – and the restored greenhouses, otherwise known as the vinery. The vinery is now a stunning new metal-framed glasshouse with three separate sections for growing every kind of crop, from tomatoes and cucumbers to aubergines and chillies.

On the outer side of the walled garden directly behind the vinery, you'll come across a series of small brick rooms that run along the perimeter. These are the early Victorian *bothies*, which were traditional working quarters for gardeners and labourers on an estate. Keep walking west and you'll reach ❸ FULHAM PALACE, an architectural treasure, which has absorbed features from the Tudor, Georgian, and Victorian periods. There's a comfortable cafe in the drawing room, looking out over the lawn. To exit the palace grounds and cross over to neighbouring Bishop's Park, follow the path that leads around the back of the palace towards Coachmans Lodge and leave through the main entrance gates to Bishop's Avenue. Once inside the park, bear left around the skatepark and you'll come to the park's main feature: an "urban beach," consisting of a bed of clean sand at one side of the lake, where locals set up deck chairs whilst children paddle around in the summertime. But the reason I've brought you here is the promenade, where you can gaze across the wide, wide river to Putney, cocooned on the other side by the park's trees, as you stroll back east along the Thames. At any point, you can press your hands against the protective stone wall and look towards the picturesque Putney Bridge, with a red double-decker London bus usually trundling into view.

Crossing the bridge, follow the curve of the pavement around to your right onto the Embankment, and you'll pass the ❹ DUKE'S

HEAD, a popular spot on boat-race day; a parade of rowing clubs; and a children's park, before reaching the towpath proper. With a mile and a half to go until the next exit, this feels more like a country walk, reminiscent of Henley rather than the city. On misty mornings, you can admire rowers out on the river, their oars cutting through the dark, grey water. Once past the London and Thames rowing clubs, you'll see a football stadium on the other side of the river. That's Craven Cottage, home to Fulham Football Club. As you follow the large bend of the river, the expanse to your left gives way to wetlands.

Soon the Hammersmith Bridge comes into view. Grade II-listed, the suspension bridge's green wrought-iron framework and cross-beams clad in ornamental cast-iron casings make it particularly attractive to the eye. Cross over here to Hammersmith for some promising diversion.

On the other side, make your way down the staircase on the left to the small parade of public houses west of the bridge. Once on the promenade, you'll pass some stunning town houses with gables and verandas, in an almost New Orleans style. Onwards a few paces, you may recognize the ❺ BLUE ANCHOR pub from the Gwyneth Paltrow movie *Sliding Doors*. As a boozer, one could charitably call it cosy, although when shoulder to elbow with some 6-foot, 6-inch rower, it can feel rather cramped. Opt for the lively terrace outside in spring and summer, and you'll likely spot a squad of scullers raising their boats high above their athletic shoulders, heading for the river. The odds are even greater that you'll pick out some Australian or South African/Zimbabwean accents, as Southwest London has proven extremely popular with Antipodeans, and no wonder. Within a few miles' radius, you'll find not only the River Thames but also Wimbledon Common, a deer park at Richmond, meadows, wetlands, and Kew Gardens.

Only a short walk away is ❻ THE DOVE pub, which boasts the best terrace for boat-race day, although only if you're fortunate enough to position yourself early on. There's even an upper deck, accessed by a spiral staircase, for those brave enough to multi-task

Left: Blue Anchor; Right: Hammersmith Bridge

climbing while balancing a tray of drinks. The chimney of the Fuller's Brewery, which has been making beer here since the 19th century, can be seen from the Dove, just a mile away to the west. The pub, situated on Upper Mall, can only be accessed via a cobbled alleyway. The 18th-century poet and Dove regular James Thomson reputedly wrote the words to "Rule, Britannia" here, whilst William Morris lived close by. Above the fireplace in the compact, dark-wooded front bar, you'll find a full list of the luminaries who have dropped in over the years. It's a real find.

To access the nearest public transport, simply retrace your steps and follow the Hammersmith Bridge Road north as far as St Paul's Centre church and follow signs for Hammersmith Station.

Above: Thames Path

STARTING POINT
Putney Bridge
Underground Station

GETTING THERE
District Line

1 FULHAM PALACE GARDENS
Bishop's Avenue
London SW6 6EA
+44 20 7736 3233
www.fulhampalace.org

2 WALLED GARDEN
Fulham Palace
Bishop's Avenue
London SW6 6EA
+44 20 7736 3233
www.fulhampalace.org

3 FULHAM PALACE
Bishop's Avenue, London SW6 6EA
+44 20 7736 3233
www.fulhampalace.org

4 DUKE'S HEAD
8 Lower Richmond Road
London SW15 1JN
+44 20 8788 2552
www.dukesheadputney.co.uk

5 THE BLUE ANCHOR
13 Lower Mall, London W6 9DJ
+44 20 8748 5774
www.blueanchorlondon.com

6 THE DOVE
19 Upper Mall
London W6 9TA
+44 20 8748 9474
www.dovehammersmith.co.uk

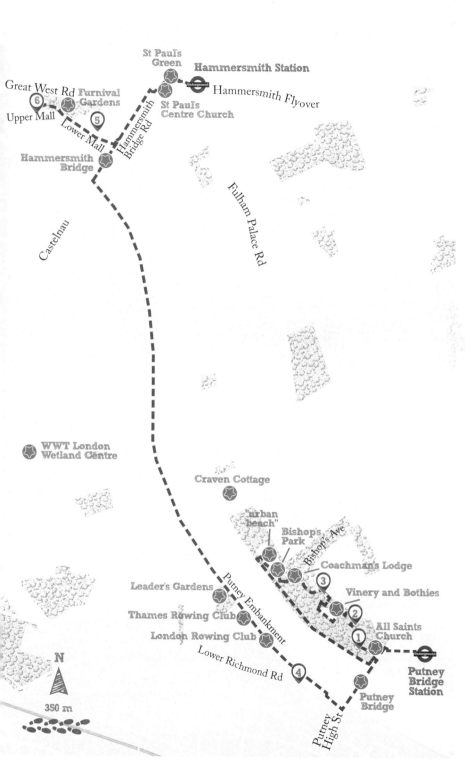

31_ The Getaway Walk

Richmond to Ham

BEST TIME: Spring or autumn
DISTANCE: Approximately 10 kilometres

For West Londoners, Richmond is our getaway; it's where we retreat when we want to reconnect with nature but only have several hours to do so. Here, we can tramp across acres of parkland or savour a scenic river walk. Few out-of-towners make it to Zone 4. So, whilst other Londoners are packing visitors and family from abroad off to Buckingham Palace or Soho, I keep this place up my sleeve for stressed-out friends swapping one city for another, bestowing upon them a moment of respite.

Exit Richmond Station, and you are in one of the loveliest suburbs of London. Richmond's history dates back to Tudor times, when, in the 16th century, Henry VII had Richmond Palace built. Whilst the palace is gone, many well-preserved listed buildings of architectural or heritage status remain. You'll get to those all in good time; first notice the view. The celebrated vista of the vale of the Thames from the summit of Richmond Hill has long been the inspiration of writers and artists, and is presently protected by a specific Act of Parliament.

Turn left out of the station and power along the attractive high street. Follow the road's bend, passing Waterstones bookstore on your left, until you reach a mini roundabout. Cross over and you'll come to a fork in the road. Bear left to continue onto Hill Rise, which morphs into Richmond Hill. From the ❶ TERRACE GARDENS, spectacularly laid out upon a steep slope, you'll have a glorious view of the River Thames – a perspective captured for posterity by the famous English landscape painter Turner. The gardens were originally formed from three separate 18th-century estates and opened as a public park

Opposite: Terrace Gardens

Clockwise from top left: Village signpost; statue in the Terrace Gardens; boats for hire on the river; view from Richmond Park; deer in Richmond Park; Petersham Meadows

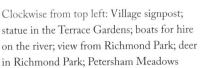

in 1887. Thanks to a recent £1 million refurbishment, they have been restored to their former glory, and residents and visitors alike can walk among the mature trees, enjoy a picnic, or simply be with nature.

Continue ascending Richmond Hill, and after the second roundabout, you'll reach the park via Richmond Gate. Created by Charles I in the 17th century as a deer sanctuary, Richmond Park is the largest of London's Royal Parks. Today, it is of national and international importance for wildlife conservation. Once inside, turn right onto the first footpath running parallel to Queen's Road. Half a mile in, you'll see a car park and signs for ❷ PEMBROKE LODGE, a Grade II-listed building that was once home to a British prime minister and his grandson, the philosopher Bertrand Russell. From the vantage point of the lodge's gardens, there are still further panoramic views of the English countryside.

To access the trail of paths that lead to the bottom of the hill, ask a staff member for directions, explaining that you are walking down to Ham. Follow the path that heads in a south-easterly direction. When it meets the path traversing the base of the hill, turn right and keep walking for 300 metres, passing the children's playground on your way, until you arrive at a gate. Exit the park here and turn left toward the Dysart pub, which is diagonally across the street, and continue along Petersham Road. Follow the bend around to your left, and when you reach Sandy Lane, turn right. You are now in the heart of Ham.

At road's end, turn right onto Ham Street and follow the signs for ❸ HAM HOUSE, a National Trust property, and the reason most visitors come all this way. Flanked by hundreds of trees stretching east to the arched gate house at Petersham and south across the open expanse of Ham Common, the house has changed little in 300 years, and the same applies to its formal gardens, which feature the oldest orangery in Britain, an icehouse, and a dairy. Be on the lookout for parakeets which nest in amongst the courtyard's walnut and chestnut trees. Inside, it is an atmospheric 17th-century time capsule.

On leaving the house and its grounds, turn right and follow the path around, passing Ham Polo Club. Should you wish to be

Left: Richmond promenade; Right: Petersham Nursery Café

a spectator and tread some divots, the polo season runs from the beginning of May to the end of September. There are matches every Sunday starting at around 2pm. Pedestrians pay as little as £2, so be sure to stock up on some *wurste* and pretzels for a picnic.

Passing the German School, turn left at Petersham Road. Follow the bend of the road to the first turning, towards Petersham Meadows. Just before reaching the meadows, stop off at ❹ PETERSHAM NURSERIES (an elegant, exotic greenhouse). For me, a real find is a place that creates a mood which is both eccentric and inviting. You'll want to see what the owners have done with the place.

Leaving the nurseries behind, keep to the footpath and cut through the pleasant Petersham Meadows, where artists have been setting up their easels for close to 300 years to paint grazing sheep (and the view, of course). If you've the time and money to splurge, then I highly recommend a detour at Buccleuch Gardens onto Nightingale Lane, just across Petersham Road. ❺ PETERSHAM HOTEL, at lane's end, isn't a place you stumble upon. You have to be in the know to find your way onto the grounds of this beautiful country hotel, which offers unspoilt panoramic views and a quintessentially English afternoon tea.

From here, bypass the shopping precinct of Richmond in favour of its waterfront promenade, which is famous for lazy summer days and evenings spent lounging on its lawns or restaurant terraces. The Grade I-listed Richmond Bridge, which is the oldest surviving bridge over the Thames in London, adds to the charm of this stretch of riverside. Before the next bridge, turn onto Old Palace Lane, where you can stop off at the historic ❻ WHITE SWAN and dip into its unseen beer garden in back before heading up to Richmond Green. Once home to kings and queens, the neighbourhood's ancient past is reflected in the names of the surrounding streets: the Wardrobe, Friars Lane, Old Palace Yard, and ❼ OLD PALACE GATE. This last is where you'll find the only remaining section of the medieval Richmond Palace: a redbrick gatehouse bearing Henry VII's coat of arms. Today, the green is surrounded by substantial Regency and Georgian houses, but in Tudor times, the houses here would have served the palace. Cross the green diagonally to Little Green, where you can dip down Old Station Passage and return to Richmond's modern train station, from whence you came.

STARTING POINT
Richmond Station

GETTING THERE
District Line (Underground)
or Overground from Waterloo Station

❶ TERRACE GARDENS
Richmond Hill
Richmond TW10 6RH
www.richmond.gov.uk

❷ PEMBROKE LODGE
Richmond Park
Richmond TW10 5HX
+44 300 061 2200
www.royalparks.org.uk

❸ HAM HOUSE AND GARDEN
Ham Street
Richmond
+44 20 8940 1950
www.nationaltrust.org.uk

❹ PETERSHAM
NURSERIES
Church Lane
Off Petersham Road
Richmond TW10 7AB
+44 20 8940 5230
www.petershamnurseries.com

❺ PETERSHAM HOTEL
Nightingale Lane
Richmond TW10 6UZ
+44 20 8940 7471
www.petershamhotel.co.uk

❻ WHITE SWAN
26 Old Palace Lane
Richmond TW9 1PG
+44 20 8940 0959
www.whiteswanrichmond.co.uk

❼ OLD PALACE GATE
Old Palace Yard
Richmond TW9 1PD

Above: View from the Terrace Gardens; Below: Isabella Plantation, a 40-acre woodland garden in Richmond Park

32   The Alternative Kew Walk

Chiswick to Kew

BEST TIME: First Sunday of the month, morning
DISTANCE: Approximately 10 kilometres

Living in Chiswick, I would while away many a Sunday morning on Strand-on-the-Green, a riverside village paradise situated east of Kew Bridge. I would gaze across the Thames from the veranda at Café Rouge whilst men in whites strode past readying themselves for an afternoon's cricket on Kew Green. As others flocked to famed Kew Gardens (300 acres of landscaped grounds and botanical glasshouses) nearby, I preferred to keep hold of the £15 in my pocket, exploring instead the more public charms of the river path, local park, and sacred car boot sale. So, sacrilegious as it may sound, the charms of Kew Gardens shall remain a mystery on this walk, an optional extra should the desire take hold.

Starting out at Turnham Green, in the heart of Chiswick, turn right out of the station onto The Avenue, pass the church, and wander the nearby streets of Bedford Park (see map on p. 357), a fashionable garden suburb where most of the properties are Victorian or Edwardian and residences range from small artisan cottages to the large Norman Shaw houses. Shaw was the leading architect of his day and explored eclectic styles ranging from Gothic Revival to Neo-Baroque to Palladian. The elegant town houses (some with balconies) you see here are adapted from the Queen Anne style. Laid out in long rows, they are differentiated by detailing in the gables, windows, and tall chimneys. Fine examples of Shaw's designs can be found at the lower end of The Avenue, whilst The Orchard has the most striking examples of one-off houses. Created as a middle-class commuting

Opposite: A typical Bedford Park house

Above: The Old Cinema antiques store; Below: The Avenue, Bedford Park

village in the 1880s, the sought-after area soon became a haven for intellectuals and artists, amongst them Henry James, Thomas Hardy, and H G Wells. Returning to the church, head south down Turnham Green Terrace for Chiswick High Road.

Today, Chiswick is still decidedly middle class, with young children trotting along to Foubert's for ice cream, whilst the grown-ups lunch around the corner at High Road Brasserie. Here, the proprietors play to Chiswick residents' sensibilities, fusing sleek design with cheeky rococo. Check out its vintage bar and Art Deco interior on your way to THE OLD CINEMA on Chiswick High Road, named one of the 100 best shops in the world by *Retail Week*. Wander through room after room, floor upon floor, browsing for antiques and vintage 20th-century furniture in this Edwardian former picture palace. This place is a tardis.

Walk east along Chiswick High Road, and it's like being on the set of a Hugh Grant movie, although you're more likely to bump into local Colin Firth. As with all the chic high streets in London though, there's always another Carluccio's or Zizzi's restaurant, Cath Kidston or Oliver Bonas retail store, so instead, burrow into those places that locals go out of their way for. For that, you'll need to turn down Duke's Avenue. At Hogarth Lane, head beneath the underpass, and, aboveground again, pass through the gates and into the grounds of CHISWICK HOUSE, a neo-Palladian villa once owned by Lord Burlington and set within beautiful historic gardens. The whole park is an oasis of meandering paths lacing through Italian Renaissance gardens.

First, follow the path and signs for the Conservatory, which was designed by Lord Burlington around 1720, and contains what is considered to be the oldest camellia collection outside of China and Japan. These magnificent blooms are at their best during February and March. To view the classically designed Palladian main house, head south in the direction of the water. From Chiswick House, the lawn slopes gently down to the lake. Imagine the picturesque garden trails around you, illuminated at night by 50 giant hand-sculpted lanterns rising into the star-lit sky. Well, locals saw this for real when

Chiswick House and Gardens hosted the Magical Lantern Festival to celebrate the Chinese New Year in 2016. From all reports, it truly was an enchanted evening as guests wandered through corridors of light. To see more classical flourishes scattered throughout the park, I urge you to head to the northernmost tip of the lake and across the elegant stone bridge. Follow the path running parallel to the lake until you catch sight of the Cascade, which is a pretty waterfall. Exit through the nearby white gate onto Burlington Lane.

Across the way on Burlington Lane is ❸ CHISWICK SCHOOL, whose car park is well worth a visit the first Sunday morning of the month. That's when residents from far and wide make their way to the popular Car Boot Sale. Set in the unassuming grounds of the local school, this event is not to be missed. Summer or winter, come rain or shine, hundreds of hardy souls are out here hunting for treasure. In cooler months, layer up and wear your wellies, as the playing field gets rather muddy. Pay the £1 entrance fee and head towards the bustling playing field first, where the antique dealers set up. Vendors begin queuing from 5am to grab a coveted spot to sell their wares. You can find anything here, from Victorian jewellery to mid-century modern furniture. Around the back of the school you'll find the more traditional car boot and household items. Press on through this area, as late-arriving antique and house-clearance merchants set up here too.

When it's time to leave, head out the Staveley Road exit and make a left and then a right onto the Great Chertsey Road. Walk on 500 metres until you reach the entrance for Grove Park and bear left, around the health club to the exit onto Hartington Road. Turn right onto Hartington and then take the first left for a quick detour to ❹ CHISWICK QUAY. The first time I stumbled upon this marina I had made a wrong turn. For months afterwards, I kept trying to repeat that same mistake, for what I discovered was something of an incongruous time capsule – a 1970s estate of town houses wrapped around the most unexpected of marinas; almost Mediterranean in aspect. Whilst I'm sure the locals would prefer to keep this to

Clockwise from top left: Signpost for Chiswick House; drawing of Chiswick House; Ionic temple, Chiswick Gardens; Bedford Park; lake at the heart of Chiswick Gardens

Oliver's Island

themselves (ensuring it is well-obscured from view behind hedges), it is just too good a find not to share.

Return to Hartington Road, which merges with Grove Park Road after 700 metres. From here, you can join the river walk on your left via Thames Road. This stretch of the Thames Path is called Strand-on-the-Green, which is also the name of the old fishermen's village it borders. One of the most picturesque, bucolic parts of London, the path is lined by numerous imposing 18th-century houses. It's home to some popular riverside pubs as well, such as the Bell and Crown and Bull's Head. My personal recommendation, though, is the ⑤ CITY BARGE, which overlooks the iron Kew Railway Bridge and Oliver's Island, a small, heavily wooded island, which derives its name from a myth that Oliver Cromwell once took refuge on it.

Crossing over the Thames on South Circular Road, you arrive at ⬤ KEW GREEN. In one corner is the old horse pond, and on a summer's evening you can look on as the local cricket club plays one of their matches. During August, a horticultural show is held on part of the green. Continue along the South Circular another 450 metres and turn left down Ruskin Avenue. Would it surprise you to know that buried in this backstreet you'll find none other than the *Domesday Book* (the most historic document in English history)? Saunter through some ominous-looking gates onto a fossilized 1970s campus, complete with man-made ponds and fountain. This rather clandestine building is home to our ⬤ NATIONAL ARCHIVES, where researchers, budding genealogists, and family history buffs have been making their way for decades. Entrance is free. When you've filled up on the past, return to the South Circular and cross over to Burlington Avenue. From here, simply follow the road around over the railway bridge to Kew Gardens BR Station.

STARTING POINT

Turnham Green Underground Station

GETTING THERE

District Line

⬤ THE OLD CINEMA

160 Chiswick High Road
London W4 1PR
+44 20 8995 4166
www.theoldcinema.co.uk

Burlington Lane, London W4 2RP
+44 370 333 1181
www.english-heritage.org.uk

⬤ CHISWICK SCHOOL
AND CAR BOOT

Burlington Lane, London W4 3UN
www.chiswickcarbootsale.com

⬤ CHISWICK QUAY

Hartington Road,
London W4 3UR
+44 20 8994 8743
www.chiswickquay.com

⬤ CITY BARGE

27 Strand-on-the-Green
London W4 3PH
+44 20 8994 2148
www.citybargechiswick.com

Richmond TW9 3BH

⬤ NATIONAL
ARCHIVES

Bessant Drive
Richmond TW9 4DU
+44 20 8876 3444
www.nationalarchives.gov.uk

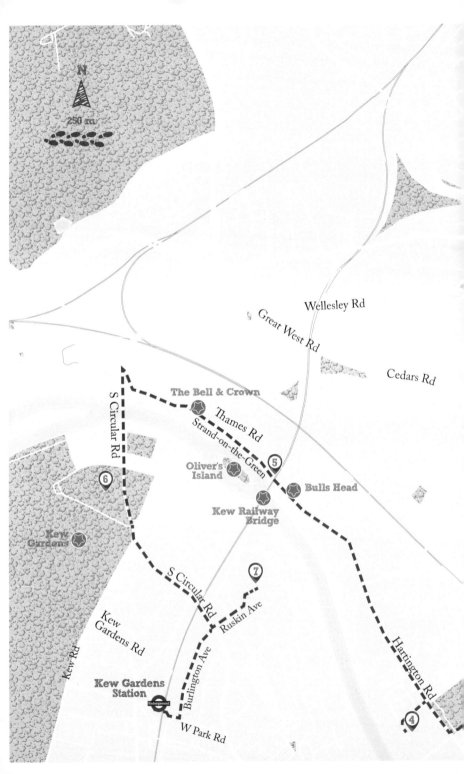

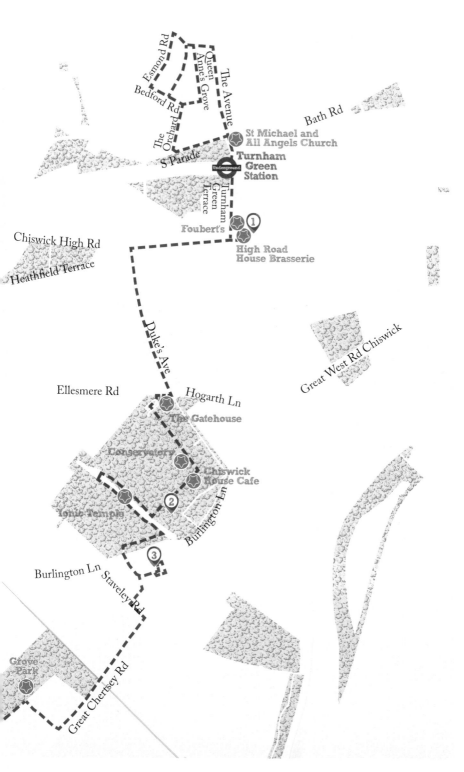

33__ The Country Walk

Hammersmith to Barnes

BEST TIME: Spring
DISTANCE: Approximately 8.5 kilometres

For many, Hammersmith is best known for the A4 flyover, a section of motorway linking the city to the west of England. But for those living and working here, this inner-city hub is a cultural smorgasbord with a wealth of pubs, shops, reputable theatres, and a world-class music venue. What makes it all the more remarkable is that in just a 20-minute walk, you can find yourself in the midst of an idyllic rural setting. For the nearby village of Barnes, in the south west of the capital, is one of London's loveliest spots, possessing all the classic attributes of country life. Sitting on a great curve of the Thames, the picture-postcard enclave lays claim to a 2.5-mile riverfront, a duck pond, weeping willows, and, inland, hundreds of acres of common land, wild fields, and even a secret cricket pitch.

Step out of Hammersmith Station at the King Street Exit, and whilst the locals flock to the high street, bear left instead towards the grounds of the large church at the centre of a maelstrom of cars and buses. Wander through the green around ❶ ST PAUL'S CENTRE to Hammersmith Bridge Road, which leads across Hammersmith suspension bridge.

Once on the other side of the Thames, head right down the ramp and you can be enjoying a woodland walk along the riverside path within minutes. Go in the spring, and this stretch is replete with a canopy of trees in blossom. Come wintertime, the scene isn't quite so affecting. Still, there's nothing like that feeling of being cocooned.

Shaded by foliage, you really get to stretch your legs along this lovely piece of river frontage. From the nature trail you can access ❷ LEG O' MUTTON NATURE RESERVE, an 8.2-hectare

Opposite: Riverside walk

Clockwise from top left: Barnes Duck Pond; The Bull's Head; The Terrace; a terrace house on Lonsdale Road; The Sun Inn; Barnes High Street sign

BARNES·HIGH·STREET

THE TERRACE S.W. 13.

BURNING SUN AND SILVER MOON
the SUN INN
SILVER FLOWING WATERS

reservoir that is a haven for birds. Cormorant, heron, tufted duck, and all manner of feathered creatures can be seen here. Bats roost in the enormous poplar trees, which date back to the 1850s.

Out in the country, it's common practice for ramblers to offer a cheery "hello" and a smile upon crossing one another's paths. Londoners find this convention foreign, preferring to avert our gazes and pretend other pedestrians do not exist. Please don't take offence; we've just been trained this way.

Back on the towpath, be on the lookout for ❸ THE BULLS HEAD, Barnes's answer to Ronnie Scott's jazz club in Soho. This period pub began featuring live jazz in 1959 and hasn't stopped since. The great and the good of the jazz world have performed here. Before you turn onto Barnes High Street, take a few moments to admire ❹ THE TERRACE on Lonsdale Road, with its elegant terraced houses, replete with porticos and verandas.

Saturday morning on Barnes High Street has a timeless feel about it as residents with proper shopping baskets visit the butchers and bakers and have coffee with friends. It's a charming village, with well-to-do locals dipping into J Seals Butchers, at No. 7, for venison or choosing between a smoked cheddar and some creamy camembert from the Real Cheese Shop, at No. 62. They even have their own honey shop, Bees of Barnes.

On Friday mornings there's a ❺ COUNTRY MARKET at Rose House and on Saturday mornings there's a ❻ FARMERS MARKET in the grounds of the Essex House.

Arriving at ❼ BARNES POND, at the end of the high street, surrounded by weeping willows and Edwardian homes, you'll feel you are in an Austen-esque England; you can just picture the families (Mama and the girls in petticoats and Papa in his frock coat) stepping out into Regency society. Incredibly, Barnes has been home to the composer Handel; the author Henry Fielding, who resided in the grand ❽ MILBOURNE HOUSE facing the pond; and Dodie Smith, author of *I Capture the Castle* and *101 Dalmatians*. ❾ THE SUN INN is a pleasant place to stop off before walking through the green and traversing the wide expanse of Barnes Common beyond.

The true wonder of postcode SW13 – a world away from Hammersmith's postcode W6 – comes when you venture onto Barnes Common, and step out into glorious countryside. Wonderfully wild, the rough beauty of this far-as-the-eye-can-see patch of dry grassland and natural woods makes it the ideal place to gather your thoughts. There are houses marooned out here and even a secret cricket green. It wouldn't remain a secret if I revealed its location, but perhaps you'll stumble upon a game as you tramp across the varied landscape of meadows, woodland, and heath. By all means, venture in as far as you like but go too far, and you'll have crossed over into Putney Lower Common.

Keeping today's walk Barnes-centric, I urge you to head up Rocks Lane for ❿ LONDON WETLAND CENTRE, a 100-acre nature reserve and ecological oasis in the heart of the capital. To reach the centre, turn right on Queen Elizabeth Walk and left at the signposted footpath. This place is a hive of habitats, with lakes and pools, wader scrapes, reed beds, grazing marshes, water meadows, and a resting site for more than 200 species of birds, many amphibians, and even some otters. At dusk, you might even spot some bats. (There is a charge to enter the wetlands, so you might want to factor that in.)

Return to Queen Elizabeth Walk, passing the intersection with Rocks Lane, and cross over onto Church Road. Given the rural location of Barnes, it may surprise you (it did me) to hear that the cinema at 117 Church Road was home to ⓫ OLYMPIC SOUND STUDIOS in the late 1960s. Considered on a par with Abbey Road Studios, where the Beatles recorded, Olympic was the go-to studio for many iconic bands, including the Rolling Stones, Jimi Hendrix, and Led Zeppelin. You really do find the strangest of things in the most unexpected places. If you're still in Barnes in the evening, you'll find a great local Italian restaurant, ⓬ RIVA, on Church Road and Castelnau, a mile-long stretch of exceptional classical villas that leads all the way back to Hammersmith Bridge and "modern" civilization.

Above: Barnes Pond; Below: Barnes Common

① ST PAUL'S CENTRE
Queen Caroline Street
London W6 9PJ
www.stpaulscentre.org

② LEG O'MUTTON
NATURE RESERVE
Lonsdale Road
London SW13 9QN
www.richmond.gov.uk

③ THE BULLS HEAD
373 Lonsdale Road
London SW13 9PY
+44 20 8876 5241
www.thebullsheadbarnes.com

④ THE TERRACE
Lonsdale Road
London SW13

⑤ BARNES COUNTRY
MARKET
Rose House
70 Barnes High Street
London SW13 9LD
+44 20 8788 7046

⑥ BARNES FARMERS
MARKET
Essex House, Station Road
London SW13 9HG
www.barnesfarmersmarket.co.uk

⑦ BARNES POND
Barnes Green, London SW13

⑧ MILBOURNE HOUSE
Station Road, London SW13 0LW
www.barnes-history.org.uk/
BandMmap/milbourne.html

Opposite: The River Thames

Above: Barnes Common

⑨ THE SUN INN
7 Church Road, London SW13 9HE
+44 20 8876 5256
www.thesuninnbarnes.co.uk

⑩ WWT LONDON
WETLAND CENTRE
Queen Elizabeth's Walk
London SW13 9WT
+44 20 8409 4400
www.wwt.org.uk

⑪ OLYMPIC SOUND STUDIOS
117 Church Road
London SW13 9HL
+44 20 8912 5161
www.olympiccinema.co.uk

⑫ RIVA
169 Church Road
London SW13 9HR
+44 20 8748 0434

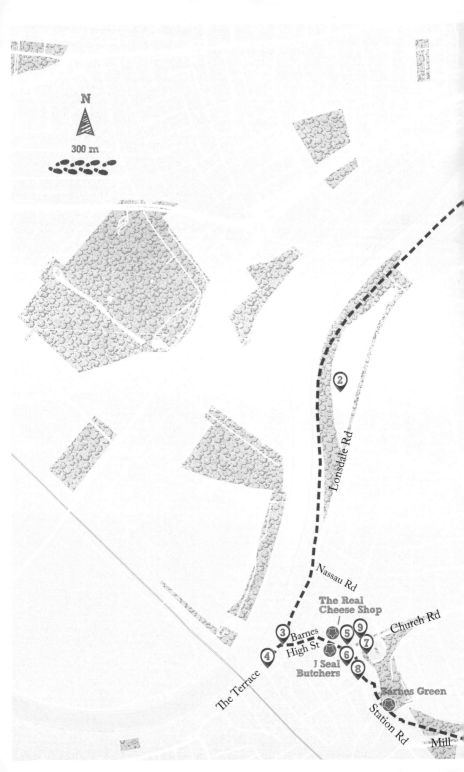

Acknowledgements

I'd like to thank Eurydice Caldwell, Vanessa Smuts, Gillian Rodney, Daniel Parisi, Simmi Bajaj, and Henrieta Arslan for helping me see London with fresh eyes; Stephanie Perry and Ian Smith for their love and support; and Katrina Fried and the team at Emons for making this book possible. – N. P.

Author

Nicola Perry was born and raised in London. Whether visiting friends, moving location every few years, or dipping into neighbourhoods through Airbnb, she loves continually exploring new pockets of the city. Professionally, Nicola has worked with writers on their creative projects for years, as book editor, storyliner, workshop leader, and storytelling consultant. She has previously worked with Amazon, Bloomsbury, and Working Partners.

Photographer

Daniel Reiter was born in Munich and works independently as a photographer in Germany and abroad. His focus is aerial, advertising, reportage, and media photography. Daniel's images have appeared in a variety of magazines, books, and advertisements. His work is represented by Getty Images, Stock4b, and Lumas Gallery.